DATE DUE

#47-0108 Peel Off Pressure Sensitive

baltimore

a picture history
1858-1968

Baltimore from Whetstone Point, 1831

baltimore

...a picture history
1858-1968
(with a prologue)

commentary by
FRANCIS F. BEIRNE

compiled under the auspices of
THE MARYLAND HISTORICAL SOCIETY

a project in celebration of the 110th Anniversary of
HUTZLER'S
Baltimore

Published by
Bodine & Associates, Inc./Baltimore, Maryland

Also by Francis F. Beirne

The War of 1812

The Amiable Baltimoreans

Shout Treason—The Trial of Aaron Burr

St. Paul's Parish, Baltimore

FOREWORD

As a centennial project for its 1958 celebration, Hutzler Brothers Company, at the suggestion of the Maryland Historical Society, sponsored the publication of *Baltimore . . . A Picture History, 1858-1958*. In the book numerous illustrations and a discerning text by Francis F. Beirne, distinguished journalist and author, sharply etched a vivid panorama of the achievement of the Monumental City as well as some of its charms, foibles and follies.

Since the issuance of that valuable work, the local scene has been far from static. During the last ten years, in fact, change probably has affected Baltimoreans and their city more startlingly than in any previous decade. To record facets of that change, Hutzler's has invited Mr. Beirne to continue his penetrating comment in this updated edition. The revision is timely, for it presents the highlights of an era during which Baltimoreans began to reshape their aspiration, to rebuild much of their city, to explore new interests, and to pursue a variety of fads and fancies. The Society has been privileged to have a part in the undertaking and extends warm appreciation to all those who have assisted.

HAROLD R. MANAKEE, *Director*
The Maryland Historical Society

Baltimore's first Courthouse overlooking Jones Falls

CONTENTS

Foreword v

Prologue (1729-1858)
    Baltimore Town—40 Shillings an Acre . . . .   1 to 25

1858-1875
    Flourishing Metropolis of the Eastern Seaboard . . . . .   26 to 51

1875-1900
    From the Somber Seventies to the Gay Nineties .   52 to 85

1900-1925
    A New Century and a Millennium That Went Astray . 86 to 119

1925-1958
    Meeting the Challenge of a Changing World . . . . 120 to 137

1958-1968
    Battle for Survival and Rebirth . . . . 138 to 185

Acknowledgments   186

PROLOGUE

1729-1858

Baltimore Town — 40 Shillings an Acre

ONE HUNDRED YEARS after its founding the Maryland colony was still largely an agricultural community. Towns were needed to serve as markets for the products of the soil and also as ports of entry where taxes could be collected on the cargoes of ships arriving in the colony, and those being loaded for voyages abroad. As centers of population and trade, towns were essential to progress and prosperity.

The colonists conceived the notion that the needed towns could be created by legislation. This got to be quite a hobby with lawmakers and land speculators. An act would be put through the Assembly at Annapolis erecting a town, and commissioners would be appointed to buy a tract of fifty acres or more. The commissioners then surveyed the land, staked it off, laid out lots, streets and alleys, and offered the lots for sale. If the venture succeeded, well and good. If it failed, another act would be put through the Assembly declaring the tract "annulled and untowned", and it reverted to its original owners.

Three towns bearing the name of Baltimore were thus erected by the Maryland Assembly. The first was on the Bush River in Harford County, and the second on the Eastern Shore. Both failed and were annulled. The third, Baltimore on the Patapsco, "took".

It was in 1729 that the Commissioners bought from Charles and Daniel Carroll a tract of 60 acres which is now the heart of downtown Balti-more. The price paid was 40 shillings an acre, in money or in tobacco at the rate of a penny a pound. Basing calculations on the price of Maryland tobacco then and now, that would be the equivalent of about $15,000 today, or less than enough to buy a modest ranch-type house burdened with the customary ground-rent.

The site of Baltimore Town was favored alike by planter, merchant and traveler because of the harbor afforded by the northwest branch of the Patapsco; the Great Eastern Road from Philadelphia to the south which passed nearby; and—odd as it may seem to us today—because of Jones Falls. In 1729 that much-abused stream provided a plentiful supply of water power, so essential to keeping the mill-wheels turning.

At the outset Baltimore Town was intended primarily as a port for shipping tobacco. But its location, as the westernmost port on tidewater in the colony, made it convenient to the wheat fields of the Pennsylvania Germans to the north and west. A test shipment of wheat to England proved profitable. So, early in its career, Baltimore became a wheat port as well as a tobacco port, a status it has maintained throughout its history.

Through these natural advantages and the energy and initiative of its people, Baltimore has grown from a modest settlement of a few scattered houses in 1729 to the flourishing metropolitan community of over a million population we know today.

A print based on John Moale's drawing of 1752

Baltimore — from Town to City

George Calvert, First Lord Baltimore

FOR WHOM was Baltimore named? There were six Lords Baltimore. George Calvert, first of the line, conceived the Maryland colony and drew up its charter; but Charles, the Fifth Lord Baltimore, was Proprietor when the city was founded.

The picture above shows Baltimore Town as it looked in 1752. In the foreground is the Basin; at the right Jones Falls. The church on the knoll is the first St. Paul's on the site of the present church. The road in the center leading down to the Basin is the present Calvert Street. Baltimore Street may be traced from left to right across the middle of the picture.

The map (right) was drawn in 1796, the year that Baltimore was incorporated as a city. Note the three original settlements—Baltimore Town (1729); across Jones Falls, Jones Town (1732); and at the far right Fell's Point, famous for shipping and shipbuilding (1733).

By act of the Assembly, Baltimore Town and Jones Town were merged in 1745. In 1773 Fell's Point was united with them, thereby ending a bitter rivalry.

*The commissioners, assisted by the county surveyor,
laying off the town on January 12, 1730*

The original town oc-
cupied a space roughly
bounded by the Basin,
Holliday, Saratoga and
Liberty Streets.

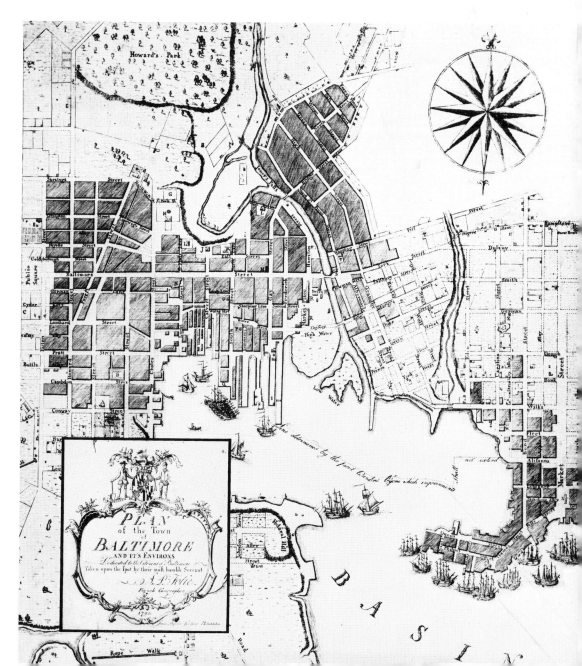

PLAN
of the Town
of
BALTIMORE
AND IT'S ENVIRONS
Dedicated to the Citizens of Baltimore
Taken upon the Spot by their most humble Servant
A. P. Folie.
French Geographer.
1792.

Baltimore in 1800. The Courthouse "on stilts", where Battle Monument now stands, solved an early traffic problem by letting Calvert Street pass under. The two-towered edifice is First Presbyterian Church (1791–1860)

At left is the courtyard at Fountain Inn, Light and Redwood Sts., opened in 1773 and long the town's chief hostelry. Washington was a frequent guest. Lafayette and Jefferson stopped here, too. Here Perry, fresh from his victory on Lake Erie, was tendered a grand banquet.

Charles Carroll of Carrollton, signer
of the Declaration of Independence

Col. John Eager Howard, hero of
the Battle of Cowpens

Revolution and Post-War Boom

BALTIMORE came through the Revolution unscathed.
The town boasted two patriots of national distinc-
tion in Charles Carroll of Carrollton, statesman, and
Col. John Eager Howard, military leader. It built
ships for the infant navy, and its gallant sons under
Maj. Mordecai Gist saved Washington's army at
Long Island.

In the post-war years trade boomed and the town
grew. The census of 1800 gave it a population of
31,514, an increase of more than 100 per cent over
the census of 1790. It was with no little pride that
the prosperous burghers set their gold watches by
the "Town Clock" in the graceful tower of the First
German Reformed Church (right). Yet on the outskirts Baltimore still bore the aspects of a village.

PEALE MUSEUM

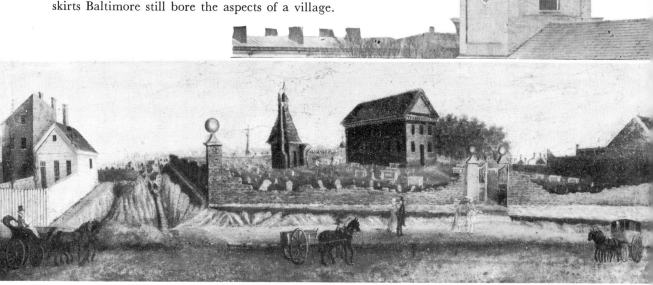

This rustic scene is Charles and Saratoga Streets, looking east, around 1800. The church is St. Paul's

5

Betsy Patterson. A pastel by D'Almaine after Gilbert Stuart's portrait

Jerome Bonaparte

Mary Caton, Marchioness Wellesley

"Glorious Betsy"—Romantic Episode

"TO MY TASTE, the women of Baltimore have more charm than the rest of the fair sex in America." Thus spoke Baron de Closen, a French visitor at the time of the Revolution. Their "white skins . . . slender figures . . . beautiful little hands . . . dainty feet" waked the gallant Baron to ecstasy.

In the next generation, queen of them all was Elizabeth Patterson, "Glorious Betsy", who won the heart and hand of Napoleon Bonaparte's brother, Jerome. Both families opposed the match but love would have its way. They were married on Christmas Eve, 1803. The romance ended when Jerome, bribed by his brother with a kingdom and a princess, basely deserted his American wife.

A rival beauty was Mary Caton, granddaughter of Charles Carroll of Carrollton. She married Betsy's brother, Robert Patterson, and after his death went to England, where she married the Marquess Wellesley, the Duke of Wellington's brother. Thus the little town of Baltimore provided sisters-in-law to the two great protagonists of the day—Bonaparte and Wellington—while the ladies were themselves sisters-in-law through Mary Caton's first marriage.

One of the lottery tickets

Mills' original design

The Monumental City

July 4, 1815, was a great day in Baltimore, when the populace marched 20,000 strong to Howard's Woods to lay the cornerstone for the first monument in the nation to George Washington. The Governor and Mayor were there and so was Robert Mills, the designer, with a painting of his column. The monument in modified form was completed in 1829. As was the custom of the day, funds were raised by lottery to the amount of $178,000. Thus Baltimore earned the title of the "Monumental City".

Robert Cary Long, the architect, made this sketch

Marshaling the troops on Hampstead Hill (Patterson Park) before the battle

"A Nest of Pirates"

IN THE WAR OF 1812 Baltimore privateers demoralized British trade by their daring raids on merchant ships that extended even to the English coast. Stung by their losses, the British vowed to wipe out that "Nest of Pirates" on the Chesapeake. Defense of the city was entrusted to Maj. Gen. Samuel Smith, a veteran of the Revolution.

Maj. Gen. Samuel Smith

September 12, 1814, British troops under Maj. Gen. Robert Ross landed at North Point and marched on Baltimore. They were met by Brig. Gen. John Stricker's City Brigade and, in the ensuing battle, Ross was killed. His death was attributed to two youthful riflemen, Daniel Wells and Henry McComas, who also lost their lives in the fight.

September 13, the British fleet bombarded Fort McHenry throughout the day and well into the night, but the garrison under Lieut. Col. George Armistead bravely held out. "By the dawn's early light", Francis Scott Key, a Maryland lawyer who had gone to the fleet to sue for the release of a friend, Dr. Beanes, saw that "our flag was still there". Thus inspired, he scribbled on the back of a letter the lines which a few days later were set to music and are now our National Anthem.

The flag which flew over the fort was made by Mary Pickersgill, whose home on East Pratt Street is preserved as a national shrine under the name of "The Flag House".

September 12, 1815, the cornerstone was laid for Battle Monument (Calvert and Fayette streets) in honor of men killed in the fight. Ever since then September 12, "Old Defenders Day", has been a public holiday.

At right, Francis Scott Key, and the flag as it looks today. Below, the first stanza of the poem in Key's handwriting.

O say can you see ~~through~~ by the dawn's early light,
what so proudly we hail'd at the twilight's last gleaming,
whose broad stripes & bright stars through the perilous fight,
O'er the ramparts we watch'd, were so gallantly streaming?
And the rocket's red glare, the bomb bursting in air,
Gave proof through the night that our flag was still there,
O say does that star spangled banner yet wave
O'er the land of the free & the home of the brave?

"—the bomb bursting in air." A print showing the bombardment of Fort McHenry by the British fleet. It was made shortly after the engagement

For Baptists who practiced total immersion, Jones Falls proved convenient

At left, the ordination of Bishop Asbury in Lovely Lane Meeting House on Redwood St., where the Merchants' Club now stands.

Archbishop Carroll

The Roman Catholic Cathedral as Benjamin Latrobe designed it, completed in 1821. The present onion towers were added later

The Seed that Fell into Good Ground

BALTIMORE holds a unique place in the religious history of the nation, appropriate to the chief city of Maryland, where religious freedom in America had its beginning.

Following the Revolution, the Pope appointed Father John Carroll, a Marylander, Vicar General of the Roman Catholic Church in the United States. In 1789 Father Carroll became the first Roman Catholic Bishop in this country. In 1808 the Baltimore Cathedral, which he had planned, was elevated to the rank of a metropolitan church and Dr. Carroll was invested with the dignity of Archbishop. Thus Baltimore became the birthplace of the Roman Catholic hierarchy in this country.

Baltimore may claim also the country's first Methodist Bishop. December 27, 1784, Francis Asbury was ordained in Lovely Lane Meeting House. At the same conference the Methodist Church in the United States was born.

Otterbein Church, on Conway Street near Sharp, erected in 1784 and the oldest church edifice still standing in the city, was named for Bishop Philip William Otterbein, on whose teaching the Church of the United Brethren in Christ was based.

In 1842, Baltimore saw the organization of Har Sinai Congregation, first Jewish congregation founded on Reform principles in the United States. This group held its first regular services in 1843 in a second-floor front room in the home of Moses Hutzler, Exeter Street and Eastern Avenue (right).

Otterbein Church

11

A busy day at the Fairview Inn on the Frederick Road, a few miles outside the city

How the Rolling Road got its name.
The hogshead contains tobacco

A Market and a Port

"THE MOST flourishing commercial town on the continent" was the comment of a visitor at the turn of the century. Every day there could be seen on the Frederick Road, the York Road and other roads leading to the city, droves of cattle and Conestoga wagons, drawn by four-horse teams with jingling bells, each laden with a ton of corn, wheat or flax, and other products from the rich farms of the Germans of Pennsylvania and Western Maryland.

Baltimore merchants purchased the supplies for local consumption or to be shipped to the northern markets, to England and to the West Indies. By 1804 there were 50 mills within 18 miles of the city making flour for shipment, while tobacco continued to be an important article of export.

Jones Falls was prized for its water power. A mill and cooperage works near the present Fallsway and Eager Street

The Iron Horse Saves the Day

AT THE VERY PEAK of its prosperity Baltimore suddenly was faced with a serious threat to its future growth. In 1825 the Erie Canal was opened, providing an unbroken waterway from the Great Lakes to New York City. It diverted valuable western trade which hitherto had gone to the port on the Chesapeake.

What was to be done? To meet the crisis, a far-seeing group of Baltimore merchants hit on the bold scheme of building a railroad all the way to the Ohio River. It seemed a mad enterprise, for railroads then were in their infancy.

On July 4, 1828, the whole town and hosts of visitors repaired to Mount Clare where, with solemn ceremony, the cornerstone of the Baltimore & Ohio was laid. Charles Carroll of Carrollton, Baltimore's "Grand Old Man", then 90 years old, turned the first spade of earth.

In 1829 the New York inventor, Peter Cooper, began to build his experimental locomotive, the Tom Thumb, at the Mount Clare shops. So uncertain was the promise of the steam railway engine that it was a question whether horses should be used instead. In the first trial the Tom Thumb broke down and the horse won.

Carrollton Viaduct over Gwynns Falls, built in 1829 and still in use. The first large masonry bridge in the U.S.A.

The Grasshopper, designed in 1832. An engine of this type was used on the first run between Baltimore and Washington, August 25, 1835

The famous race between the Tom Thumb and a horse car on August 28, 1830. The horse won

LOTTERY
AND EXCHANGE OFFICE,

S. E. Corner of Baltimore street & Market space,
BALTIMORE,

They got up to $50,000

Pleasures of fox hunting

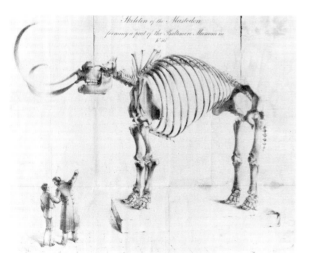

The Peale Museum's Mastodon

Sports and Other Diversions

"ALL WORK and no play makes Jack a dull boy" is a popular philosophy among Baltimoreans. In the early days they did not lack opportunity to enjoy their leisure.

In sports the horse ruled supreme. Flat racing attracted crowds to Canton, Whetstone Point and other nearby tracks. Fox hunting was enthusiastically pursued—sometimes with disastrous results. There was duck and railbird shooting on the marshes, and excellent fishing in local waters.

Amusements were varied. On occasion the town turned out for the thrill of a balloon ascension. But for steady fare the public depended on the theater. A favorite among the playhouses was the Holliday Street, Baltimore's "Old Drury Lane". The doors were opened at 4:30 P.M. and the show began at 6:30 P.M. To save time at the box office, patrons were warned to bring the right change. Here half-mad Junius Brutus Booth delighted audiences with "King Richard III". The sword play in the Battle of Bosworth Field was better than a Western. Opened in 1813, the Holliday Street Theater served the public for over a century, eventually descending to melodrama and burlesque.

Balloon Ascension in Fairmount Park in 1834. The Shot Tower, Cathedral and Washington Monument are seen in the background

Then there was Rembrandt Peale's Museum with its wonderful collection of beasts and birds, alive and stuffed. Patrons stood open-mouthed before the skeleton of the mastodon, dug up in New York State by the Peales.

There were no $64,000 quiz programs in those days. But lotteries offered as good a chance to get rich quick. Note the luck of the anglers in the upper left-hand corner.

Holliday Street Theater. This building was destroyed by fire in 1873, but was soon rebuilt

AMERICAN TURF REGISTER, 1830

Railbird shooting on the marshes

A view of the harbor around 1840. Ships plying to bay and river points, as well as ocean-going vessels, swelled the traffic.

Enter the Baltimore Clipper

DURING the French Revolution and the wars which followed, Baltimore shipping came into its own. A prime factor was the Baltimore clipper (left). This trim schooner-rigged vessel, with her two masts sharply raked and a hull designed to slip swiftly through the water, was the speediest craft afloat. She carried the United States flag and Baltimore's fame throughout the seven seas. By 1827, flour represented more than half the exports, while coffee, brought in from Brazil on return voyages, was to make Baltimore one of the nation's leading coffee ports by the middle of the century.

In 1797 Capt. David Porter built an observatory on Federal Hill. A telescope picked up incoming ships at North and Bodkin Points. Signal flags notified ship owners across the Basin who had crews ready to unload and thereby saved time and money on insurance.

Belvidere, built in 1786–94. The picture shows the garden front as it looked around 1858

Typical town houses on Howard Street, near Baltimore, in 1820

HUGHES COMPANY

Mount Clare, from a recent photograph

Homewood, on North Charles Street

Monuments to Gracious Living

FROM the earliest time, Baltimoreans have had an innate love of the soil. They have not been content to stay cooped up in the city if they could afford a country place outside. Soon the town was ringed by large estates, each with a handsome mansion. As Baltimore expanded, these estates were swallowed up, often leaving only their names behind to identify neighborhoods.

The earliest example which still survives is Mount Clare, built by Charles Carroll the Barrister in 1754. Now fully restored, it stands in Carroll Park. Another noble survivor of the Georgian period is Homewood. Built by Charles Carroll of Carrollton for his son, Charles Jr., it serves as the administration building of Johns Hopkins University. John Eager Howard's imposing home, Belvidere, overlooked the town from an eminence northeast of Mount Vernon Place until the mansion was torn down to make way for the extension of Calvert Street.

Town houses, erected in rows, were less pretentious. Yet they too managed to present to the world an air of comfort, hospitality and graciousness.

ALL PICTURES ON THESE PAGES, EXCEPT AS NOTED, FROM THE MARYLAND HISTORICAL SOCIETY

PEALE MUSEUM

PRIZE TALE.

BY EDGAR A. POE.

MS. FOUND IN A BOTTLE.

A wet sheet and a flowing sea.

CUNNINGHAM.

Of my country and of my family I have little to say. Ill usage and length of years have driven me from the one and estranged me from the other. Hereditary wealth afforded me an education of no common order, and a contemplative turn of mind enabled me to methodize the stores which early study very diligently garnered up. Beyond all things the works of the German moralists gave me great delight; not from any ill-advised admiration of their madness, but from the ease with which its rigid thought enabled me to ...

MARYLAND HISTORICAL SOCIETY

MARYLAND HISTORICAL SOCIETY

At left, Edgar Allan Poe. Above left, *The Saturday Visiter*, of Oct. 19, 1833, featuring the prize story, "Ms. Found in a Bottle". Above, Poe's grave in Westminster Presbyterian churchyard.

Literary Flowering

MARYLAND HISTORICAL SOCIETY

The Delphian Club Celebrating their
First Anniversary. —

Illustration from the Delphian Club minutes

IN THE EARLY decades of the 19th Century, Baltimore was the scene of an outburst of literature. Between 1815 and 1833 no fewer than 72 periodicals were started here. Among the budding authors was Edgar Allan Poe, who made his home in the city from 1831 to 1835 and returned here to die. In Baltimore he won a $50 prize for a short story. "Distinguished by a wild, vigorous and poetical imagination", said the judges, who included John P. Kennedy and J. H. B. Latrobe, themselves authors. A biographer comments: "For the first time his name was associated with success."

A meeting place of writers, artists, scientists and wits was the Delphian Club, which assembled weekly at the home of a member to feast and play. Active or honorary members were the authors of three immortal songs—Francis Scott Key (*The Star Spangled Banner*), John Howard Payne (*Home, Sweet Home*) and Samuel Woodworth (*The Old Oaken Bucket*).

REMBRANDT PEALE, DEMONSTRATING IN PEALE'S MUSEUM, BALTIMORE, THE APPLICATION OF GAS LIGHTING WHICH INAUGURATED THE GAS INDUSTRY IN AMERICA, JUNE 13, 1816.

Rembrandt Peale's gaslighting demonstration

The Peale Museum

The tape bearing the famous message in the Morse Code

Gaslight and Telegraph

IN JUNE, 1816, at his museum, before an awed company that had paid a small admission fee, Rembrandt Peale demonstrated illumination by carbureted-hydrogen gas. A "very brilliant and pleasing light", reported the *Baltimore American* of June 14. Five days later the City Council granted to the Gas Light Company of Baltimore permission to light the streets. Chartered in 1817, this was the first gaslight company in America.

Twenty-eight years later Baltimore was the scene of another epoch-making event when, on May 24, 1844, in the old B. & O. station, at Pratt and Light Streets, the famous message "What Hath God Wrought!" came over Samuel F. B. Morse's electromagnetic telegraph from the Supreme Court room in the national capitol in Washington. Interestingly enough J. P. Kennedy and J. H. B. Latrobe, who had encouraged Poe, also aided Morse.

Professor Morse and the instrument he invented

19

Monument Square, 1848

City Spring, at Calvert and Saratoga Streets

Medical College, University of Maryland, Lombard and Greene Streets. Designed by R. C. Long, Sr. (1812)

Baltimore in 1837, viewed from the present Chase Street near the Fallsway

Landmarks Past and Present

FROM 1815, when Maximilien Godefroy's memorial to the Old Defenders was dedicated, Monument Square was a popular place for mass meetings, military pageantry and an occasional riot. This was literally the "Court End" of the town, beginning with the "courthouse on stilts" and ending with the imposing courthouse of today.

A block to the north was the City Spring, "a spacious fountain where clean cold water, gushing fresh from the spring, ran gurgling over a channeled floor of marble".

In 1837 the Baltimore skyline, viewed from the north over Jones Falls, presented a charming panorama. From left to right the eye took in two Shot Towers and the Jail, the Clock Tower, First Presbyterian Church, the Court House, Cathedral and Washington Monument.

The Exchange, designed by Benjamin Latrobe and Godefroy, was for half a century the most significant structure in the city. Here merchants and shipowners met daily to trade. Here were the Custom House, a bank and post office. In the rotunda, on their passage through the city, the bodies of Henry Clay (1850) and Abraham Lincoln (1865) lay in state. The Exchange was torn down in 1901 to make way for the new Custom House.

Two surviving landmarks are the building of the Medical Faculty of the University of Maryland, and the Shot Tower, last of three, in which shot was made by dropping molten lead from the top into tanks of water below.

The Merchants' Exchange, Gay Street

The Shot Tower (erected 1828)

The burning of Webb's warehouse on Howard Street in the early morning of March 18, 1827. Two firemen lost their lives when a gable fell in on them.

A hook and ladder company of the olden days

The Independent Fire Company Tower still dominates the scene at Gay and Ensor Streets

They Fought Fires and Each Other

Mechanical, Mercantile, Union, Friendship, Liberty, Independent, Vigilant, New Market, Columbian, Franklin, Washington, Patapsco, Howard, and *Watchman* were the names of volunteer fire companies that reached the peak of their activities in the 1840's. So keen was the rivalry among them that fires were deliberately started to see who could get there first. Frequently the race ended in a free-for-all in which bricks from the sidewalks and cobblestones from the streets provided ammunition. Our firemen and political hoodlums combined to give Baltimore an unsavory reputation throughout the nation as "Mobtown". A paid fire department was organized in 1858. It inherited the old rivalry. Every boy had his favorite engine company, and even in the late nineties the challenge was still heard, "What engine do you go for?"

The homely scene at the right adorned the cover of "The Hard Cider Quickstep", a popular campaign tune published in Baltimore. The doughty hero of Tippecanoe gives a war veteran a hearty handshake.

The Great Whig Convention of 1840

MIDWAY BETWEEN North and South and convenient to the national capital, Baltimore was a popular place for holding party conventions. One of the most famous was the Whig Convention of 1840, which met to ratify the nomination of William Henry Harrison and John Tyler. The great day was May 4, when a parade formed at the center of the city and marched through decorated streets to Canton Race Track.

There a crowd of 20,000 was addressed by Daniel Webster, Henry Clay and other Whig titans.

In contrast to his opponent, Martin van Buren with his drawing-room manners, Harrison was portrayed as a battle-scarred hero of the frontier. "Tippecanoe and Tyler, Too" was the Whig slogan, and the Log Cabin and Hard Cider figured prominently. Harrison won by 234 electoral votes to 60.

The political meeting at the Canton Race Track on May 4, 1840

A bird's-eye view of the city in mid-century

The City in the 1850's

"A DELIGHTFUL PLACE, either for a man of bustle and business, or a man of quietude and pleasure; for the one will find himself in a flourishing port of entry, of immense traffic, of numerous manufactures, and about the largest market for tobacco and flour in the Union, while the other may enjoy all the advantages of its several literary and scientific institutes, roam about the exquisite scenery of the surrounding country, or at the proper season go and revel in the far-famed sport of duck-shooting. . . .". Such was a discerning visitor's comment in the year 1853.

By this time downtown Baltimore had assumed an aspect that is familiar to Baltimoreans of today. Howard's Woods had been converted into Mount Vernon Place, a formal square on which fronted commodious dwellings. Some of them survive to the present time. Though a century has passed since the print above was made, no one could doubt that the community over which the Father of His Country stands watch so benignly is Baltimore.

This broad and gracious avenue is Broadway as it looked in the 1850's; then as now the main thoroughfare of Fell's Point.

MARYLAND HISTORICAL SOCIETY

Looking north on Liberty from Baltimore, St. Paul's rectory and the Catholic Cathedral in the background. Stepping stones were needed when a downpour flooded the street.

PEALE MUSEUM

When it snowed the hill on East Lexington Street afforded fine coasting. The old court house is at the left. The date is 1856.

ENOCH PRATT FREE LIBRARY

Baltimore and the inner harbor as viewed from Federal Hill in 1857

Flourishing Metropolis

1858-1875

By 1858 BALTIMORE had grown from a provincial town to a metropolis. While it had yielded second place to Philadelphia, it was still the third largest city in the nation, with a population of 212,418.

The two decades following the depression of the 1830's had witnessed great prosperity. In 1857 the city was securely linked to the Mississippi Valley when the B. & O. reached St. Louis. A distinguished party from Baltimore made the first trip. Soon after, a delegation from St. Louis returned the visit and enjoyed a fabulous banquet at the Maryland Institute.

The sleek clippers which had carried Baltimore's overseas trade at the turn of the century were now replaced by the clipper ships. These were designed to preserve some of the speed of their predecessors, but on a greater scale, to accommodate the heavy cargoes of flour and tobacco that went out to foreign ports in enormous quantities. They brought back equally large cargoes of coffee, hides, sugar, guano and copper from the West Indies and South America. Still

e Eastern Seaboard

other vessels plied regularly between Baltimore and the ports of Chesapeake Bay and the South. To the southern ports went fertilizer, of which the city was becoming a big producer, and manufactured goods. Returning vessels brought raw cotton to feed Baltimore's textile mills, while Baltimore bankers and merchants were the chief extenders of commercial credit to the South.

A primary factor in Baltimore's population growth was the arrival of thousands of immigrants, chiefly from Germany and Ireland. Their numbers and their demands alarmed some native Americans, who organized themselves into the American, or Know-Nothing Party. The Know-Nothings' favorite weapon was terrorizing the foreign voters to keep them from the polls. Baltimore's bloody elections grew into a national scandal. At last responsible citizens rose in revolt, cleaned out a corrupt police force and restored order and decency.

Other events of 1858, testifying to Baltimore's new status as a metropolis, were the modernizing of the police and fire departments, including the adoption of a police and fire alarm telegraph system, and the establishment of a clearing house by the banks. Dr. Thomas Buckler appeared before the City Council with a bold proposal for filling up the Basin, from Light Street to Jones Falls, which incurred much ridicule from the wiseacres. That year saw also the incorporation of the Peabody Institute, the Towsontown Railroad Company and the Maryland Club.

In the midst of this wave of prosperity, Baltimore was faced with the specter of what William H. Seward called "the inevitable conflict" between North and South. The city's position was especially painful because of its strong ties with both sections. While the vast majority of its people deplored secession and the destruction of the Union, on the other hand they were equally determined in their opposition to the use of force against the Southern States. Soon Baltimore was to be a house divided.

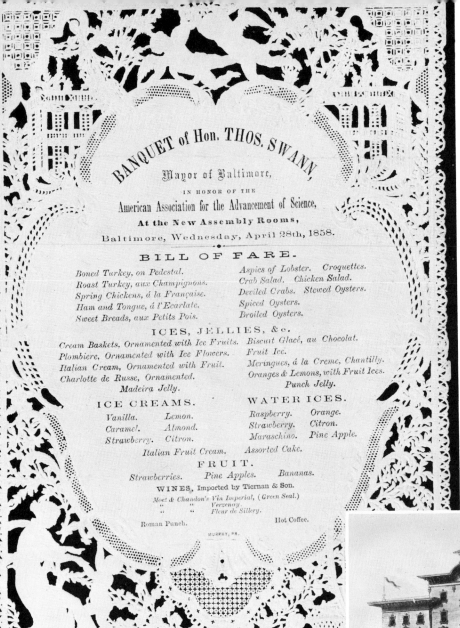

BANQUET of Hon. THOS. SWANN,

Mayor of Baltimore,

IN HONOR OF THE

American Association for the Advancement of Science,

At the New Assembly Rooms,

Baltimore, Wednesday, April 28th, 1858.

BILL OF FARE.

Boned Turkey, on Pedestal.
Roast Turkey, aux Champignons.
Spring Chickens, à la Française.
Ham and Tongue, à l'Ecarlate.
Sweet Breads, aux Petits Pois.

Aspics of Lobster. Croquettes.
Crab Salad. Chicken Salad.
Deviled Crabs. Stewed Oysters.
Spiced Oysters.
Broiled Oysters.

ICES, JELLIES, &c.

Cream Baskets, Ornamented with Ice Fruits.
Plombiere, Ornamented with Ice Flowers.
Italian Cream, Ornamented with Fruit.
Charlotte de Russe, Ornamented.
Madeira Jelly.

Biscuit Glacé, au Chocolat.
Fruit Ice.
Meringues, à la Creme, Chantilly.
Oranges & Lemons, with Fruit Ices.
Punch Jelly.

ICE CREAMS.

Vanilla.   Lemon.
Caramel.   Almond.
Strawberry. Citron.

Italian Fruit Cream.

WATER ICES.

Raspberry. Orange.
Strawberry. Citron.
Maraschino. Pine Apple.

Assorted Cake.

FRUIT.

Strawberries.   Pine Apples.   Bananas.

WINES, Imported by Tiernan & Son.

Moet & Chandon's Via Imperial, (Green Seal.)
"   "   Verzenay.
"   "   Fleur de Sillery.

Roman Punch.   Hot Coffee.

MURPHY, PR.

It was in the year 1859 that Oliver Wendell Holmes, the "Autocrat of the Breakfast Table", called Baltimore "the gastronomic metropolis of the Union". The bill-of-fare was modest for the times.

SUNPAPERS

Where Terrapin Went Walking

BARNUM'S HOTEL, founded in 1825 by David Barnum (not P. T., the circus man), spread Baltimore's fame for good living throughout the civilized world. "The most comfortable of all hotels . . . in the United States", wrote Charles Dickens, a guest in 1842. It was at Barnum's, no doubt, that he shared with Washington Irving that "enchanted julep which held out far into the night".

Here were entertained Presidents John Quincy Adams, Andrew Jackson and Martin Van Buren.

Daniel Webster spoke from the steps, and from a balcony Jenny Lind, the "Swedish Nightingale", waved to an adoring crowd before her concert in December 1850, for which seats were auctioned at $100 apiece.

Here in a brick courtyard diamond-back terrapin were regularly exercised before being served up at the hotel's table d'hote dinner, priced at $1.50.

This noble institution closed its doors in 1889 and was razed to make way for the Equitable Building.

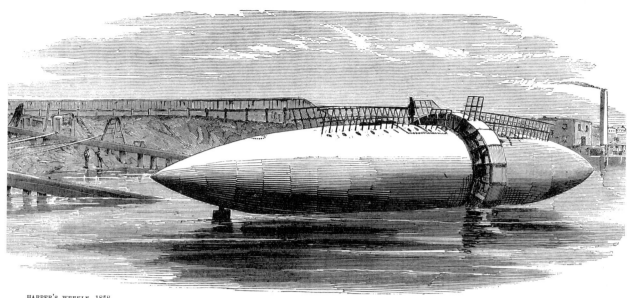

HARPER'S WEEKLY, 1858

The Winans Steamship after being launched

Daring Ideas Ashore and Afloat

THE YEAR 1858 saw the establishment of a paid fire department and the introduction of the first steam fire engines. One of these was the "Comet", made in Philadelphia and purchased for $3,400.

The same year the Cigar Ship was launched at Locust Point, on the Patapsco. Conceived by Ross Winans, who helped Peter Cooper design the "Tom Thumb", it was built by his son Thomas. The inventors dreamed of crossing the Atlantic in four days. The steam fire engines were an immediate success; the Winans with their streamlined ship were a century ahead of their time.

Thomas Winans went to Russia to make railway equipment for Czar Nicholas I. He returned in 1851 a millionaire and built Alexandroffsky, a palatial mansion set in a garden adorned with classical statuary. His staid Victorian neighbors were shocked by the undraped figures, so Winans built a 12-foot wall around his garden. Alexandroffsky was a landmark in West Baltimore until torn down in 1927.

Alexandroffsky, which stood at Baltimore Street and Fremont Avenue

"The Comet", all set to go

ALL PICTURES ON THESE PAGES, EXCEPT AS NOTED, FROM THE MARYLAND HISTORICAL SOCIETY

The *General Stricker*, a bark built in Baltimore in 1857, was a typical coffee clipper. Here she is seen leaving the local port for the run to Rio.

Industry and Commerce in 1858

TWO PRODUCTS that contributed largely to Baltimore's prosperity in 1858 were coffee and sugar. From 1825 to 1860 coffee from Brazil was the most valuable import, and ships were built expressly to carry it.

Sugar was a natural feature of Baltimore's West Indian trade. By 1858, with the erection of two new refineries, annual imports had grown to more than 8,500,000 pounds, a substantial amount then.

With this prosperity there came a demand for more retail stores, especially those catering to the needs of the women of the community. Among the new dry goods houses was that of M. Hutzler and Son, on North Howard Street, which opened its doors in 1858.

In 1858, too, a refinery guarded the harbor

This modest establishment was the first Hutzler store

30

Election Day, 1858

The City Guards leaving Boston

Transportation, Troops and Toughs

ON JULY 12, 1859, in spite of opposition from backward lookers, the City Passenger Railway placed the first rail horsecar in operation on Broadway. Soon the system was extended throughout the city.

The militia continued to lend color to the local scene. A smart outfit was the Baltimore City Guards. In 1859 it paid a visit to Boston where it was hailed as "a fine body of men . . . their drill admirable". In the Civil War the Guards was among organizations which remained loyal to the Union.

A less admirable feature of the time were the elections, when political clubs bearing such names as "Plug Uglies", "Rip-Raps", and "Tigers" terrified the voters. In the election of 1856 eight persons were killed and 250 wounded. At last an aroused public organized a reform party, drove out the rowdies and restored order. In the election of 1860 Baltimore boasted that not a shot was fired.

The first rail horsecar

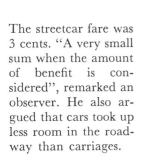

The streetcar fare was 3 cents. "A very small sum when the amount of benefit is considered", remarked an observer. He also argued that cars took up less room in the roadway than carriages.

A charming young couple of 1860

Mr. George Stewart Brown, banker, civic leader and sportsman par excellence, accompanied by Mrs. Brown, driving a tandem of spanking white horses through the gates of his estate, Mondawmin.

Dedication of Druid Hill Park

LESLIE'S WEEKLY, 1860

Union Festival. The world and his wife were there

Calm Before the Storm

WHILE THE war clouds gathered and tempers North and South rose over the issues of States' Rights, slavery and secession, Baltimoreans seized upon the last brief moment to enjoy the fellowship of community gatherings and the tranquil pleasures of domestic life before the storm broke.

A gala event was the Union Festival, held on May 24, 1859, in the Maryland Institute, for the benefit of the Young Men's Christian Association, which had been founded in England in 1844 and established in the United States in 1855. "General arrangements of the room were excellent and the decorations beautiful" said a contemporary account. A band in the resplendent uniform of the Independent Blues provided music. It was a decorous party, however, which broke up at the respectable hour of 10 P.M.

Of greater moment was the formal dedication of the new Druid Hill Park on October 19, 1860, in the presence of "an immense concourse of men, women and children" and with a military display of "an unusually imposing character". Mayor Thomas Swann delivered the oration and 4,000 school children sang an ode composed especially for the occasion by the gifted J. H. B. Latrobe, a park commissioner. The dedication ended with a salvo of artillery which drew cheers from the boys, screams from the girls.

A contemporary artist's conception of the events of April 19. Actually the scene of the bloodiest rioting was Pratt and Commerce Streets

A wartime photograph of Union troops on Federal Hill. According to local tradition, General Butler warned that, in the event of trouble, he would put his first shot into the Maryland Club, a hotbed of Southern sympathizers.

Hetty Cary

A Female Secessionist Flaunting Her Colors. "The men dare not insult the troops," said Harper's Weekly in which this picture appeared, "but the women of Baltimore presume upon their sex and wear secession colors."

"The Despot's Heel"

FOR BALTIMORE the Civil War truly began on April 19, 1861, when the 6th Massachusetts Infantry, 1,200 strong, in answer to President Lincoln's call for volunteers, passed through Baltimore on its way to Washington. Here these troops were assailed by a throng of Southern sympathizers. In the fight which followed, thirteen Baltimoreans and four men of the 6th Massachusetts were killed.

The North cried out for revenge. On May 13 a strong Federal force, under Gen. Benjamin F. Butler, seized Federal Hill and trained its guns on the town. From then throughout the war Baltimore was in fact a captive city. Yet a large part of the public continued to express their sympathy for the South.

Meanwhile, in far off Louisiana, James Ryder Randall, inspired by the city's defiance, wrote his stirring "Maryland! My Maryland". In Baltimore, Hetty Cary, a local belle, and her fair sister Jenny, set the words to music and sang them at the next meeting of "The Monument Street Girls". The song, an immediate hit, has held its popularity to this day.

An early copy of "Maryland! My Maryland"

Boston infantry and artillery take possession of Monument Square in anticipation of an uprising following the arrest of Marshal Kane and the Police Commissioners

The Mayor and the Marshal

Two MEN who played heroic parts in attempting to quell the riots of April 19 were Mayor George William Brown and Marshal of Police George P. Kane. At risk of his life plucky Mayor Brown, umbrella in hand, marched at the head of the Massachusetts troops until the situation became hopeless. Marshal Kane used the police as best he could to protect them. Yet it was on these two men that the North vented its wrath. They, along with the Police Commissioners and prominent Southern sympa-

thizers, were thrown into Fort McHenry. Later Mayor Brown, Kane and other Baltimoreans were removed to Fort Warren, Boston.

Meanwhile Baltimore became an armed camp. Federal troops patrolled the streets and fortifications ringed the city. Excitement reached fever pitch in June, 1863, when Lee's army invaded Pennsylvania and Baltimore appeared in danger of capture. The crisis ended with Gettysburg. The only Confederates to reach Baltimore were the wounded and prisoners.

Above, citizens barricading the streets on June 29, 1863. Center, Fort Marshall, on the present site of Highland-town. Below, a redoubt in Druid Hill Park, looking toward the city.

Above, dedication of the Wildey Monument on North Broadway. The building in the middle background is the Church Home. At right, this quaint structure housed Western High for 38 years (1858–1896). It stood on Fayette Street near Paca.

Return to Peace

WITH THE END of the war and the fall of the Confederacy, the nation began the long and tedious task of healing the wounds that had been opened during four years of internecine strife. Nowhere was the challenge keener than in Baltimore, in which loyalties had been fairly evenly divided.

An early gesture of conciliation attended the unveiling of the monument to Thomas Wildey on September 20, 1865. Wildey organized the first American lodge of Odd Fellows at Fells Point in 1819 and was known as the Father of Odd-Fellowship in the United States. The event took the form of a grand reunion of fraternal feeling among brotherhood members from North, South, East and West.

One of Baltimore's proud boasts is that it was the first city in the nation to establish publicly supported high schools for girls. These were Eastern and Western High, whose history begins in 1844. Both survived the strains of the war to continue their invaluable services to the young women of the city.

A City Hall Built Without a Scandal

As the City Hall looked in 1875

A FEATURE of the post-war revival was the building of a new city hall commensurate with the growth of the city. The old Peale Museum had long been too small to serve that purpose efficiently. The cornerstone was laid on October 18, 1867. "It was", said an eyewitness, "altogether a dull affair, little interest being manifested in the proceedings." This despite the fact that J. H. B. Latrobe lived up to his reputation as public orator by delivering an eloquent address. The imposing finished structure, designed by George Frederick, was dedicated October 25, 1875. Unlike so many similar undertakings, this enterprise was marred by no breath of corruption. The cost, $2,271,000, was $228,865 within the appropriation.

The laying of the cornerstone, in front of the Federal Court Building

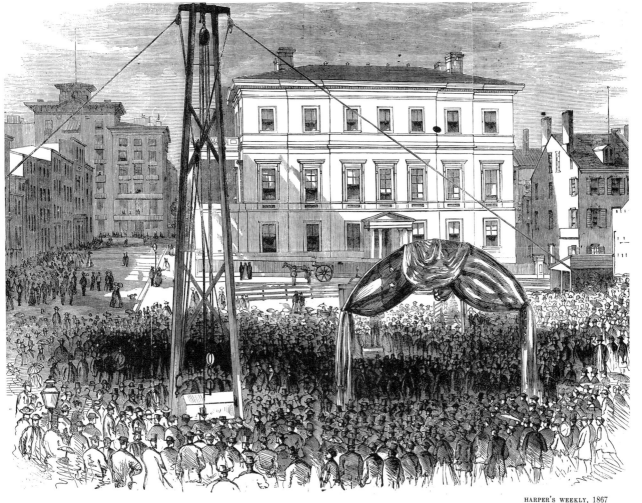

MASQUERADE BALL OF HARMONY CIRCLE

NEW ASSEMBLY ROOMS, MARCH 1ST 1866.

PEALE MUSEUM

A contemporary print. Note the "Freedmen's Bureau" in the foreground

Circle, Bunds and Lodges

WITH THE anxieties and privations of the war years behind them, Baltimoreans set to work with a will to satisfy their gregarious instincts. There were few indeed who did not belong to some group organized to promote social activities.

One such group was the Harmony Circle, a social society, which held a gala masquerade ball in the new Assembly Rooms on March 1, 1866. Costumes

were elaborate and many carried out puns. Thus the Friedman family, making use of a Federal agency very much in the post-war public conscience, came as "The Freedmen's Bureau", bureau and all.

The German population of the city, now grown to massive proportions, was, with true German thoroughness, the most socially organized of all. A conspicuous center of German activity was Concordia Hall, home

Prize singing of the Northeastern Saengerbund in the hall of the Maryland Institute on July 12, 1869

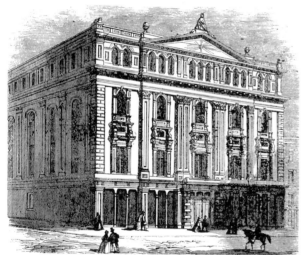

The new Masonic Temple, 1866

Concordia Hall

of the Concordia Society. Founded in 1847 as a German library, the Concordia soon extended its operations to other intellectual pursuits. Its music and drama divisions became famous. Famous also were the Saengerbunds, or singing societies, which joined with those of other cities in saengerfests, or song festivals, lasting several days. Baltimore acted often as host to the national and regional meetings.

The Masonic Order had been conspicuous in Baltimore since a very early time. Having laid the cornerstones for churches, monuments, numerous public buildings and even for a railroad (the B. & O.), it now laid one for its own new edifice on North Charles Street, in the presence of a great company including President Andrew Johnson. This building, with a few additions, has been its home ever since.

41

Library of the Peabody, completed in 1878. Note the cast-iron work for which Baltimore was famous

George Peabody (1795–1869)

The west building, designed by E. G. Lind and completed in 1861

Mr. Peabody and His Institute

"MAY NOT THIS Institute be a common ground where all may meet, burying former differences and animosities, forgetting past separations and estrangements, weaving the bonds of new attachments to the City, to the State and to the Nation."

Such was the wish expressed by George Peabody at the dedication of the west building on October 25, 1866. As a youth of twenty, Massachusetts-born Peabody set up a clothing business in Baltimore. Here he made his first $5,000, and lived for two decades before going to London to amass a great fortune. Grateful to Baltimore, which had given him his start, Peabody contributed $1,500,000 to the establishment of the Institute which bears his name.

For over a century the Peabody Institute, with its Library of rare books, and its Conservatory of Music, has proved to be an important factor in the cultural life of the community.

The steamer "Baltimore" tied up at Locust Point

*Calvert Station, built in 1855, razed in 1950
to make way for the Sun building.
The Northern Central Railroad also was
an important link with the outside world*

Hands Across the Sea

TWO EVENTS took place in the 1860's to link Baltimore with Europe. The first was the sailing of the British steamer *Somerset* from the local port on September 30, 1865, inaugurating a regular service between Baltimore and Liverpool. But the line proved unprofitable and was soon abandoned.

Lasting success, however, attended the regular steamship line between Baltimore and Bremen, Germany, which was opened with the arrival here on March 26, 1868, of the steamer *Baltimore* of the North German Lloyd. This was a continuation of a lucrative trade between the two cities that began in sailing ship days. From Baltimore went cargoes of tobacco, cotton, naval stores and coffee. From Bremen came boatloads of immigrants. In 1867 alone, over 10,000 landed at Locust Point.

The arrival of the steamer *Baltimore* was the occasion of a great civic and military celebration, including what Baltimoreans loved so dearly—a parade. An exciting feature of this was a spectacular mounted division of 350 butchers in black suits and white aprons.

*The sailing of
the "Somerset"*

In 1888 flat racing at Pimlico was suspended and not resumed until 1905. During the interval trotting races were held.

Spring Meeting.

1873. 1873.

MARYLAND
JOCKEY CLUB
AT
PIMLICO COURSE.
NEAR BALTIMORE.

Tuesday, May 27th.
First Race—2 Miles over 8 Hurdles.
Second Race—Preakness Stakes, 1½ Miles.
Third Race—Handicap Stakes, Mile Heats.
Fourth Race—Dash of Three Miles.

Wednesday, May 28th.
First Race—One and a half Miles.
Second Race—Chesapeake Stakes, 1½ Miles.
Third Race—Mile Heats, 3 in 5.
Fourth Race—Dash 2½ Miles.

Thursday, May 29th.
First Race—1½ Miles for three-year olds
Second Race—Pimlico Stakes, 2 Mile Heats.
Third Race—Free Hand cap Stakes 1½ Miles
Fourth Race—Dash of FOUR

Friday, May
First Race—Dash 1½ Miles.
Second Race—Handicap Race,
Third Race—Consolation Purse
Fourth Race—*Grand Steeple C*

Pimlico and the Preakness

DURING THE Civil War racing in Maryland went into a decline. After the war, thanks to the efforts of a great sportsman, Governor Oden Bowie, the Maryland Jockey Club was revived. A new track was built on the outskirts of Baltimore on an estate called Pimlico, from which the track took its name. The first meeting was held in the Fall of 1870 and the feature race, the Dinner Party Stakes, was won by M. H. Sanford's bay colt, Preakness. In May, 1873, a new race for 3-year-olds was established and named for the Sanford colt. The Preakness, run each Spring between the Kentucky Derby and the Belmont Stakes, has become a classic of the American turf.

Above, race card for the Spring meeting May 27, 1873, containing the first running of the Preakness. Right, an artist's conception of a race in the track's early years.

Edwin Booth (1833–1893)

Ford's Grand Opera House in the old days

An Opera House, but No Opera

ONE OF THE OLDEST theaters in the country in continuous use was Ford's, on West Fayette Street. It was built by Baltimore-born John T. Ford, who also owned Ford's Theater in Washington where Lincoln was assassinated. According to tradition, to escape that unpleasant association, Ford called his Baltimore property Ford's Grand Opera House, though it was seldom used for grand opera. The theater opened on October 2, 1871, with James W. Wallack in "As You Like It". He was the first of many distinguished actors who have appeared on that stage, a list that includes such famous names of the past as Joseph Jefferson,

Stuart Robson and Adelaide Neilson; and such notables of the present as Tallulah Bankhead and the Lunts. "The building is provided with all the elegant conveniences of the most finished theater in this country", said a contemporary. It was torn down in 1964.

Intimately associated with the Baltimore stage was the ill-fated Booth family, established by Junius Brutus Booth. Of the elder Booth's sons, Edwin won international fame. His distinguished career as a tragedian was briefly interrupted following the death of Lincoln at the hand of his brother, John Wilkes Booth.

As Howard Street looked 95 years ago

Views from a Church Spire—1873

In 1873 the steeple of the First Presbyterian Church, Park Avenue and Madison Street, was nearing completion and the scaffolding was still up. William H. Weaver, a photographer, seized the opportunity to take pictures of the city from high in the air. Boldly climbing to a platform near the summit, he pointed his camera in all directions and made a series of photographs, leaving to future generations a record of what Baltimore then looked like.

Three of Weaver's photographs are reproduced here. At the top of the page is a view looking toward Howard Street, with Monument Street houses in the foreground. Behind them is the picturesque garden of the Convent of the Visitation, inclosed by a brick wall, at Howard and Center streets. Facing Center Street is the City College; and, to the south, the Academy of Music. Both were under construction at the time the photographs were made.

On the opposite page are shown, at the top, a view of Mount Vernon Place, with East Baltimore in the background; and, at the bottom, a view looking northeast from Cathedral and Read Streets.

The Washington Monument, Mt. Vernon Place Methodist Church and the Peabody give this picture a present-day look. The long roof seen behind the church is the train shed at Calvert Station.

In the foreground is the Albion Hotel, and at the extreme right the original Emmanuel Church tower; near the top of the picture the Christ Church steeple. Note in right background the Belvidere mansion, Greenmount Cemetery and the open country beyond Jones Falls.

BALTIMORE SCHUETZEN-PARK.

One of the larger Schuetzen parks. In the 1880's one society had a membership of 1,500 families. It is said that when members and guests assembled on gala occasions they often numbered 20,000

Golden Age of the Parks

IN THE DAYS when the horse provided the only transportation in the city, before the movement to the suburbs had begun, and practically all Baltimoreans lived in row houses in town, they depended on parks for recreation and an occasional breath of air. Druid Hill Park achieved popularity soon after its opening. Those who could afford a stable came out on horseback or in every sort of equipage to enjoy a ride through the miles of shaded, winding driveways. The less well-to-do arrived at the entrance by the street railway lines. In fact the park was looked upon as such a revenue producer that a tax on every fare was one condition of granting a charter.

Favorite resorts of the German-Americans were Schuetzen parks, homes of the shooting societies which reached their peak in the decades following the Civil War. Their activities were by no means confined to the target ranges, however. A Schuetzen park was in fact a country club with dance floors, bowling alleys, and banquet rooms. There were picnic grounds too, and on holidays thousands of Baltimore's large German population made use of these facilities.

The boat lake as it looked some 90 years ago. The solemnity of the scene is no doubt due to the fear that if anybody so much as smiled it might spoil the picture.

The Mansion House in those days stood alone in all its glory. The reflecting pool has long since vanished. So have the sweet young things in crinoline, and the frock-coated cop in his rakish summer hat.

In dry weather the roads in the park got dusty. But the management just got out this trusty sprinkler. Posing for a photograph those days was as novel as appearing on TV. The Mansion House staff knew they were making history.

Locust Point was a busy spot in the 1870's as it is today. Note the grain elevators and the trainloads of coal indicating Baltimore's position as a port for bulk cargoes.

A Candid Camera in the 1870's

ON THESE PAGES are scenes that would have been familiar to Baltimoreans in the 1870's who got around their city. Locust Point, where the B. & O. Railroad delivered its shipments from the Middle West to merchantmen in the harbor for transportation overseas, was a beehive of activity.

The quaint little engines that looked like toys packed both speed and power. In the great fire of July 25, 1873, which burnt out several blocks in the Howard, Saratoga, Liberty Streets and Park Avenue area, a train bringing fire engines from Washington made the 40-mile run in 39 minutes.

Harris Creek, which entered the Northwest Branch of the Patapsco south of Patterson Park, still boasted enough water for the building of ships.

Belvidere Bridge, an ingenious piece of workmanship in wood, consisting of one arch with a 190-foot span, carrying two cartways of 12-foot width and two footways of 6-foot width, won the admiration of more than one visitor.

A locomotive of the Northern Central, vintage 1873

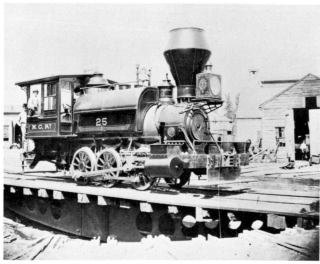

PEALE MUSEUM

PEALE MUSEUM

50

A shipyard on Harris Creek, where David Stodder built the *Constellation* in 1797. The creek has long since filled up.

Belvidere Bridge, over Jones Falls at Guilford Avenue, withstood every flood for more than 50 years.

51

From the Sombe

1875-1900

TEN YEARS AFTER Appomattox, Baltimore had recovered from the worst effects of the Civil War and regained much of its trade with the South. Old businesses and industries expanded, while new ones were added. Occasional periods of depression, like that of 1877, halted progress only temporarily.

The advent of the electric streetcar in the middle 1880's enabled the population to spread out more widely from the center of town. Suburban develop-

The lithograph shows, to the left, Locust Point and Fort McHenry, and to the right, Canton and the Lazaretto lighthouse. The upper left-hand and right-hand corners are, respectively, Camden Station and Calvert Station

venties to the Gay Nineties

ments sprang up in Catonsville, Mt. Washington and Walbrook. Yet the move to the suburbs was slow. The popular residential neighborhood continued to lie to the north and west of Mt. Vernon Place. East Baltimore, swelled by the steady flow of new arrivals from abroad, grew prodigiously.

For recreation Baltimoreans turned to picnics in the parks, boat trips down the Bay, performances at half a dozen theaters and baseball at Union Park,

where the Orioles were making history. Now that a stepladder was no longer required to mount one of them, bicycles were in high favor with women as well as men.

Sanitation was still primitive. Typhoid fever and diphtheria took a heavy toll annually. These visitations were accepted as acts of Providence, with little awareness that research in the new medical school on Broadway was in hot pursuit of the offending germs.

Here, the 6th Maryland Regiment is fighting its way through the mob. The drawing, which appeared in *Harper's Weekly* of August 11, 1877, was made from a photograph taken on the scene by David Bendann.

Violence and Calm

REMINISCENT of April 19, 1861, was a clash between citizenry and soldiers in the summer of 1877. The depression of that year forced the B. & O. Railroad to reduce wages; a strike followed, accompanied by rioting in Cumberland. Governor John Lee Carroll ordered the 5th and 6th Regiments from Baltimore to restore order. On the march from their armories to Camden Station they were stoned by strike sympathizers, and in the bloody battle which ensued, the 6th killed ten persons and wounded as many more. That ended the regiment's career.

Better times saw an end to internal strife, and in 1880 all the town united in a nine-day celebration of the 150th anniversary of its founding. All public buildings, places of business and 30,000 private houses were decorated and ten triumphal arches were raised. A conspicuous feature of the celebration was a mammoth parade in which 2,000 vehicles and 30,000 men participated; while, say the chroniclers, 300,000 persons looked on.

The townspeople were not always fighting, as the serene picture above shows. The place is Eutaw and Saratoga Streets around 1880. Below, one of ten sesquicentennial arches, looking south on Sharp Street from Redwood.

Scene at a ball held in the Academy of Music during the spring of 1880. Note the elaborate chandelier which was the Academy's great boast, along with central heating. At such balls the young ladies frequently were provided with cards (left) in which they wrote the names of their partners for each dance.

Left, in the Eighties, Fort McHenry was a popular objective. Industry had not yet changed the landscape. In spite of the advent of the Academy, Ford's continued to enjoy popularity. Below, the program for Joseph Jefferson in "Rip Van Winkle", a perennial favorite.

Social Life and the New Academy

An important addition to Baltimore's theatrical and social activities was the opening, on January 5, 1875, of the Academy of Music near the intersection of North Howard and Centre Streets. This new playhouse was declared to be one of the finest in America.

The Academy was not restricted to the drama. A false floor could be erected over the sloping orchestra seats to convert it into a ballroom. The official opening featured an inaugural ball, and the theater was frequently used thereafter for the same purpose.

The Academy overshadowed its neighbor, the infant Johns Hopkins University. It was not uncommon for visitors inquiring for the University to be told it was "near the Academy". The Academy also served as the University's auditorium.

Here on September 12, 1876, took place the formal opening of the University's first session, the guest speaker being Thomas Huxley, disciple of Charles Darwin, who had recently shocked the religious world with his Theory of Evolution. Thus Hopkins' great president, Daniel Coit Gilman, followed up his declaration of faith that science had nothing to fear from religion nor religion from science. Though an indignant newspaper editor warned that there could not be a greater heresy than Huxley's appearance, every seat was filled.

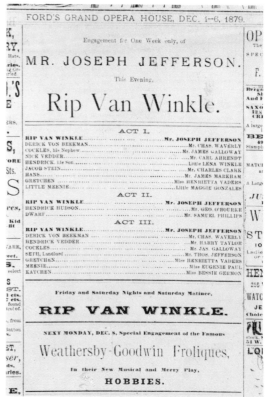

A Latrobe stove

A hitching post

Iron fountains, such as the one shown here, stood on many street corners, furnishing water for man and beast. Street pumps were the earliest form of public water supply—note the pair below.

Period Pieces

ON THESE PAGES are presented quaint objects that were a vital part of the vanished "Horse and Buggy Age". Some, like the Latrobe stove, are a childhood memory of many today. The stove, invented by that versatile Baltimorean, J. H. B. Latrobe, had a coal grate which heated a downstairs room and a flue which carried hot air to the room above, thus introducing the principle of central heating.

Does the statue of George Washington on the store front below look familiar? It's the same one that stands in Druid Hill Park. Three generations of Walkers provided clothes for Baltimore men and boys. When their store on East Baltimore Street closed in 1893, the family gave the statue to the city. Enoch Pratt supplied a new niche, which was needed because the statue has no back.

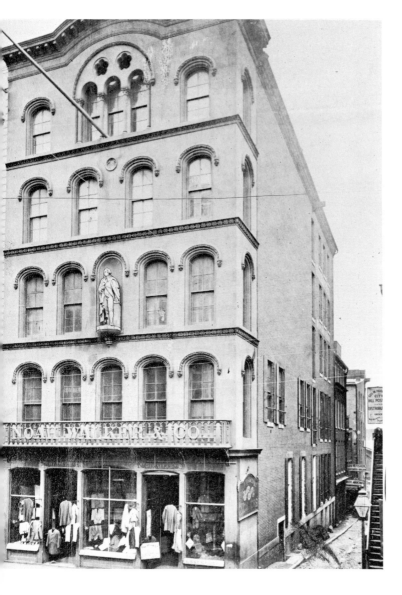

The wooden Indian that stood in front of almost every tobacco store needs no introduction.

This scene, showing newly arrived immigrants, recalls Baltimore's importance as a port of entry during the Eighties.

This old print, circa 1879, is said to depict Baltimore's first floating grain elevator. It was located at Canton.

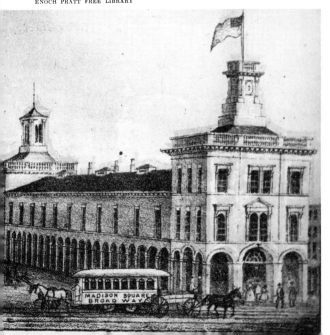

The Maryland Institute

THE MARYLAND INSTITUTE's building on Marsh Market Space, erected in 1851, was long the center of the city's intellectual life. Its large hall was in constant demand for public meetings, bazaars and party conventions. Here Millard Fillmore and Franklin Pierce were nominated. The hall also served for Baltimore's popular diversion, the lying-in-state of deceased persons of distinction: Elisha Kent Kane, arctic explorer (1857); the boy heroes of 1812, Daniel Wells and Henry McComas (1858) on the way to their final resting place in Ashland Square. The building, with the Institute's fine library, was destroyed in the Great Fire of 1904.

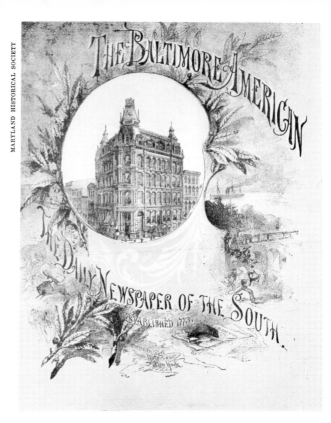

The Fourth Estate

IN NO OTHER Baltimore enterprises has the mortality been as high as in local newspapers. Of the many ventures during the 19th century the only survivors are *The Baltimore American*, *The Sun* and *The Baltimore News*. Of these the oldest is *The American*, which on May 14, 1799, in the words of its editor Alexander Martin: "like a friendless stranger threw itself before the generosity of the public". During the Civil War it was a staunch supporter of the Union, and for years thereafter the organ of the Republican Party. *The Sun* was founded in 1837 by Arunah S. Abell and now publishes morning, evening and Sunday editions. *The Evening News*, founded in 1872, and now combined with *The American*, continues under the name of *The Baltimore News-American* and Hearst ownership.

This handsome home of "The American", at Baltimore and South Streets, was destroyed in the Great Fire

The Sun, too, boasted a palatial home in its famous Iron Building, at Baltimore and South Streets. Here is a scene in its newsroom in 1885. Note the magnificence of its appointments, even down to spittoons.

SUNPAPERS

The athletic costumes above evidently were designed to set off the figure to advantage

Life with Father

MUCH HAS BEEN written about Baltimore's beautiful women. But why overlook Baltimore's handsome men? Here are presented a few sample specimens. The members of the police force pictured above believed in physical fitness and were ready to go to almost any extreme to attain it, whether by swinging Indian clubs and dumbbells, wrestling or practicing the manly art of boxing. But see the result. Even their mustaches look formidable.

Don't sell the gentlemen at the left short. They are oyster canners. With other members of their cult, in the 1879–1880 season, they packed 3,769,353 bushels raw and 2,689,939 hermetically sealed. No wonder they look so quietly self-confident.

In the sanctity of the home the father's word was law. But he was a benevolent despot who tempered justice with mercy. The contented family groups to the right testify to the happiness of those over whom the father ruled.

This good gentleman is justly proud of his wife and of his six comely daughters.

As soon as the photographer is through, the youngsters will no doubt go for a spin on their bikes, 1880 model.

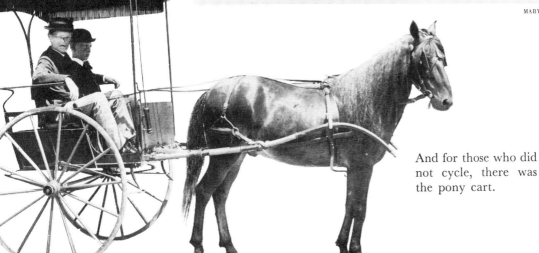

And for those who did not cycle, there was the pony cart.

First electric streetcar. To a boxcar containing a motor was attached an ordinary passenger horsecar. A third rail supplied the electric current

First Electric Streetcar and a Descendant

ON AUGUST 10, 1885, Baltimore saw the opening of the first commercial electric street railway in the Western Hemisphere. The pioneer unit, named the Faraday, ran from the present Howard and 25th Streets to University Parkway and Roland Avenue. But there were operational difficulties; people and animals got shocks from the third rail, and the line reverted to horsecars.

Of the Faraday's successors none held a warmer place in the hearts of Baltimoreans than Dolores, the funeral car. She made her debut in 1898, plying between bereaved homes and the cemeteries. "Moving on tracks where there is no jolting wipes out an objection made by many to attending funerals", observed the railway company.

Dolores all ready for a run

Above, Enoch Pratt (1808–1896). Right, the first central library building on Mulberry Street.

ENOCH PRATT FREE LIBRARY

The Historical Society and the Pratt

MARYLAND HISTORICAL SOCIETY

TWO INSTITUTIONS that have long played an important role in the intellectual life of the city are the Maryland Historical Society and the Enoch Pratt Free Library.

The Historical Society was founded February 1, 1844, its object being "to collect, preserve and diffuse information relating to the civil, natural and literary history of Maryland, and American history and biography". Its activities center around its library and museum, and include lectures and historical publications.

In 1882 Enoch Pratt, a merchant transplanted from Massachusetts, offered the city a library building and cash to the total value of $1,058,333.33, provided the city paid $50,000 annually toward the upkeep. The offer was accepted and, on January 5, 1886, the central library opened with 28,000 books. The collection has since grown to some 1,850,000 volumes and the number of cardholders to more than 300,000.

The Athenaeum stood at St. Paul and Saratoga Streets. A gift from the people of Baltimore, it housed the Historical Society from 1848 to 1919.

65

One of Kinnier's buses. Note the musicians on top and the Japanese lanterns

Picnics

PICNICS were a popular form of entertainment in the Eighties and Nineties. Among people of fashion a tablecloth spread on the ground, wines and other delicacies served by a butler, gave tone to the party. Picnickers used their own equipages to reach the picnic ground.

Those who had to depend on public transportation could charter a bus from George Kinnier. Kinnier's buses were fabulous affairs of unbelievable length drawn by four horses. Longitudinal seats provided ample room for thirty or more passengers. Singing and general gaiety made the trip to and fro the best part of the party. Buses, too, were the usual transportation for athletic teams from their hotels to the parks. It took a skillful driver to handle these long vehicles in the narrow streets.

A smart picnic party

Fertilizer, Bristles and Beer

HERE ARE ILLUSTRATIONS of the diversification of Baltimore industry in the 1870's and 1880's. Conspicuous is the fertilizer trade, which began with regular shipments of guano from Peru in 1840. With the shift to chemical fertilizer, the Baltimore area became a leading producer and still is.

Nationally important in the production of hair goods was the William Wilkens Co. The brewing industry, always present on the local scene, was producing from 700,000 to 800,000 barrels annually when Prohibition came along in 1920 and took it temporarily out of business.

Above, a tempting beer "ad" of the 1870's. Right, this plant was absorbed by the present American Agricultural Chemical Company.

The Wilkens factory, on Frederick Avenue, covered 15 acres. Employes' houses occupied 150 acres adjacent. In 1880 Wilkens was turning out 40,000 pounds of manufactured goods a week.

JOHNS HOPKINS HOSPITAL

Above, view from the southeast of the Johns Hopkins Hospital and grounds as they appeared on the opening day, May 7, 1889. Right, Johns Hopkins (1795–1873). Below, John Singer Sargent's familiar painting of "The Four Doctors"—William H. Welch, William S. Halsted, William Osler and Howard A. Kelly.

ENOCH PRATT FREE LIBRARY

PHOTOGRAPH BY HARRY B. LEOPOLD

Johns Hopkins' Great Bequest

JOHNS HOPKINS, born of a Quaker family in Anne Arundel County, came to Baltimore and made a fortune as a merchant and banker. As early as 1867 he decided to use it to establish a university and a hospital, both of which were incorporated in that year. The bequest, estimated at $7,000,000, became effective after his death, when his will was probated in 1874. The hospital on North Broadway, for which the founder himself selected the site and bought the land, was opened in 1889. The medical school followed in 1893, and, with the assistance of President Gilman's sage counsel, at once attracted a group of brilliant young men under whose leadership it achieved world-wide fame.

This quaint structure, at Aisquith and Orleans Streets, was the home of Eastern High from 1870 to 1906.

Next, a College for Women

MENTION has been made of that bold adventure in women's education—the establishment of Eastern and Western High Schools. Having had this taste of knowledge the women were not happy until they could go to college, just like the men. But those who guided the destiny of the new Johns Hopkins University were reluctant to let down the bars.

A solution came in 1884 when the Baltimore Conference of the Methodist Episcopal Church recommended the "founding and endowment of an institution of the first grade for the higher education of women". The Woman's College of Baltimore opened on September 17, 1888. Its guiding spirit was the Rev. John F. Goucher, president from 1890 to 1908. On his retirement the name was changed to Goucher College in his honor.

The Woman's College of Baltimore (now Goucher) on St. Paul Street, as it looked around 1895

Union Station about 1900. It served the Pennsylvania, Northern Central and Western Maryland. This station was razed to make way for the present Pennsylvania Station, opened in 1911.

The Ellicott City line had a standard gauge of 4 ft. 8½ ins. Normally Baltimore gauge was 5 ft. 4¼ ins., to conform to that of horse-drawn wagons.

Transportation Progress

A GREAT ADVANCE in speeding north-south railway travel in the 1870's was the digging of the Wilson Street and the Union tunnels, enabling trains to pass straight through the city. Prior to that the coaches had been drawn by mules between stations. At the same time Union Station on North Charles Street was erected.

Another ambitious undertaking was the building of the North Avenue Bridge to span Jones Falls Valley and four railway lines. This remarkable feat of engineering was constructed entirely of masonry without reinforcement, and with no power save hand power. It took six years (1891–1897).

Meanwhile the streetcar lines were extending out into the country. One line ran from Saratoga Street to Ellicott City in the expectation of eventually going all the way to Washington.

The North Avenue Bridge under construction about 1897. The picture was taken from the bank of Jones Falls.

Steamboats and Tobacco

No BUSIER or more congested spot could be found in town than the Light Street wharves before the Great Fire. Light Street then was a narrow thoroughfare through which horse-drawn wagons struggled to make their way with incoming and outgoing freight. The steamboats that docked here were links between Baltimore, the Chesapeake Bay country and the South, where a profitable trade flourished. The city served as a supplier of manufactured goods on the one hand, and as a ready market for farm produce on the other.

On East Conway Street, adjacent to the docks, were the state tobacco warehouses and hogshead market. Here were sold at auction the Maryland and Ohio crops, chiefly for export to Germany, Holland and France. In 1895 exports totaled in the neighborhood of 68,000,000 pounds.

*Hogsheads of tobacco outside the warehouses,
waiting to be inspected*

Light Street around 1885

The championship Orioles: Top row—Joe Quinn, John McMahon, Charley Esper, George Henning, Frank Bowerman, William Clarke, James Donnelly. Middle row—Walter (Steve) Brodie, Bill Hoffer, Joe Kelley, Mgr. Ned Hanlon, Wilbert Robinson, Hughie Jennings, Henry Reitz. Bottom row—Jack Doyle, John J. McGraw, Willie Keeler, Doc Pond, Mascot Sam.

Orioles, Ariels and Arundels

THE HIGH POINT in Baltimore sports was reached in the days of the old Orioles, champions of the National Baseball League in 1894, 1895 and 1896. Under the skillful leadership of Edward Hanlon ("Foxy Ned") and with such star performers as John McGraw, Wilbert Robinson, Hugh Jennings, Steve Brodie and Wee Willie Keeler, they provided a brand of baseball that some critics claim has never been equaled.

Almost simultaneously, Baltimore athletes were displaying their prowess on the water, organized into two rowing clubs—the Ariel and the Arundel—popularly known as "the Patapsco Navy". The Clubs were established respectively in 1864 and 1898. Their clubhouses on the Middle Branch were adorned with trophies won in eights, fours and single sculls in Middle States regattas. Last public mention of the Ariel was made in 1927. The Arundel continued for some years as a social club.

These stout Ariel Club crewmen could more than pull their weight in the boat

The *Louise*, on a fine day with a crowd aboard and flags flying, sails for Tolchester. She was used on moonlight nights, too.

Recreations: Summer and Winter

WHAT BALTIMOREANS of the older generation do not remember the steamer *Louise*! Built in Wilmington, Del., in 1864, she began her romantic local career in 1883 when she was bought by the Tolchester Line. For more than 40 years the *Louise* was the city's favorite excursion boat, plying between Baltimore and the Eastern Shore resort. For countless children, whose reward for Sunday school attendance was a picnic to Tolchester, the *Louise* was a happy incident along the road to salvation. In 1925 she was sold north and eventually sank in Sheepshead Bay.

The boat lake at Druid Hill Park has been an equally popular source of recreation. In many a winter cold snap, the news, "Ice on the lake in Druid Hill", flashed by word of mouth across the town, has sent skaters hurrying there.

Skaters on the boat lake at Druid Hill. The picture was taken on New Year's Day, 1895.

73

The Carrollton, at the southeast corner of Baltimore and Light Streets, occupied most of the block. The date of this view is 1890.

The Eutaw House at Baltimore and Eutaw Streets. This photograph was taken in the 1880's when the hotel was at the height of its fame.

Above, the Rennert, at Saratoga and Liberty, in 1900. Note the Belgian blocks, which succeeded cobblestones. St. Paul's Rectory is at the left.

Three Famous Hostelries

AFTER SERVING the public for close to a century, the Fountain Inn was torn down. Even before that, plans had been laid for another hotel on the same spot. In 1872 the Carrollton opened its doors, boasting an elevator, and guest rooms connected with the central desk by "galvanic fluid", as electricity was then called. The hotel burned in the Great Fire of 1904.

The Eutaw House, only ten years younger than Barnum's, opened for business in 1835. Here General Robert E. Lee stayed while visiting Baltimore after the Civil War. Later the Eutaw House was the home of the old Orioles and visiting baseball teams. There being no locker rooms at the ball park, the teams dressed at the hotel and made the trip to the park in one of George Kinnier's buses. The hotel, a mere shadow of its former self, disappeared in 1914.

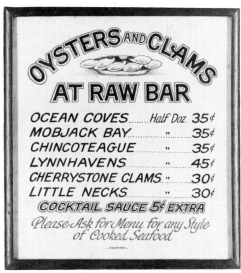

For years the Rennert was the city's leading hotel. Its cooks were skilled at preparing such typical Maryland delicacies as terrapin, duck and oysters. It was famous, too, as headquarters of the local Democratic party and its picturesque boss, Sonny Mahon. Founded in 1875 by Robert Rennert, it continued in operation until 1939. The raw bar sign above was rescued the night of the closing.

75

Left, Saratoga and Howard around 1900. Note the hospitable swinging doors to the tavern, and the ice wagon at far right. Below, a busy shopping day at Hutzler's when bodices and bustles were the mode. Inset, Joel Gutman's, around the corner on Eutaw Street.

This Was North Howard Street

FASHIONABLE shopping center, theater district, university, locale of small merchants in miscellaneous retail trade, with an occasional tavern thrown in for good measure—such were the ingredients that contributed to the throbbing activity of North Howard Street in the last decades of the 19th Century. From Baltimore Street on the south to Richmond Market on the north, and from dawn to the small hours after midnight, there was not a moment of repose. No wonder that, with this odd assortment of neighbors, the infant Johns Hopkins was sometimes lost to sight.

BOTH PICTURES FROM LESLIE'S WEEKLY, 1888

·JOEL·GUTMAN·X·CO·

·INTERIOR·OF·HUTZLER·BROS·STORE·

Above, two residences thrown together served as the earliest administration building of Johns Hopkins University.

Right, looking east on Little Ross Street. Levering Hall, at left, was put on jacks and rolled a half block uphill to Eutaw Street to make room for McCoy Hall, while the public gasped and marveled.

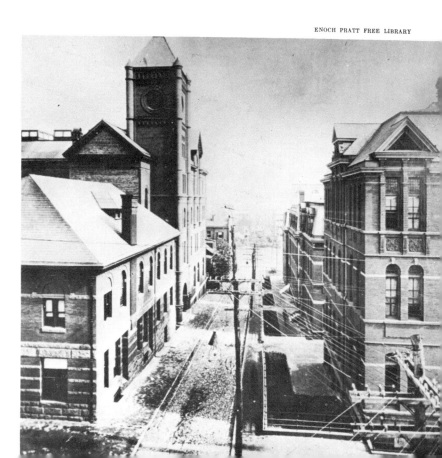

These men (1897) wear the black and blue jerseys typical of the early Hopkins athletic teams. Some of the players no doubt stayed on to help win the intercollegiate lacrosse championship in 1898

Hopkins Banjo Club, 1896. The handsome young man seated at the extreme left is Albert C. Ritchie, later Governor of Maryland.

An art class at the Woman's College (not yet re-named Goucher) sketches from a living model.

A group of Loyola students costumed for the play, "William Tell". The time is 1893.

"Golden Haze of Student Days"

A CONSPICUOUS feature of student activities has always been the group photograph, taken for the yearbook, or used to adorn a locker room wall, or bought and treasured by the individual as a souvenir of school or college. Here are four that have come down from the 1890's, illustrating respectively athletics, music, theatricals and art.

No American college boasts a more continuous history of lacrosse than does Johns Hopkins, where it has been played since 1888. In the early days the players wore no protecting helmets, and in Baltimore for years a broken nose was the distinguishing mark of the veteran lacrosser. But the Hopkins under-graduate was versatile. Having risked his skull on the athletic field in the afternoon, he showered down, parted his hair in the middle, donned white tie and tails; and, in the evening, as a member of the banjo, mandolin or glee club, charmed the fair sex.

The Woman's College, too, had its undergraduates who celebrated their new emancipation by engaging in rough sports in the gym, but without interference with the pursuit of art. Contemporaneously, youths at Loyola took time off from their Latin studies to exercise their talents in drama.

The Queen Louise Fete. Left to right: Virginia Mc-Intosh, Cumberland Rumbold, Virginia Atkinson, Tom Harrison, Harry Lehr, Lota Robinson, John Stewart, Bland Saunders, Jimmy Sykes, Vera Jenness.

Right, Harry Lehr as he appeared in a Paint and Powder show in the 90's. Another Paint and Powder star was Reese Cassard (above left) whose specialty was ballet.

Above, judging four-in-hands at the Elkridge Kennels in 1898. Right, a vehicle characteristic of Baltimore in the 90's was a barouche, drawn by two horses. The cost—about $1,500.

Theatricals and Horse Flesh

IN THE NINETIES Baltimoreans went in for private theatricals with gusto. The Wednesday Club, on North Charles Street, and the drama branch of the Concordia Society staged plays throughout the winter season. Young people of fashion favored elaborate spectacles, such as the Queen Louise Fete of 1896, in which costumes were chosen expressly to show off the belles and beaux to the best advantage. This too was the golden age of the Paint and Powder Club, which annually put on a musical show with an all-male cast. A moving spirit in these activities was Harry Lehr,

distinguished as a female impersonator. This irrepressible youth with a feminine companion once startled staid Baltimoreans by wading through the Mt. Vernon Place fountain in evening dress. Lehr was shortly to win national fame entertaining Newport society with a "monkey dinner" and other merry pranks.

While Henry Ford out in Detroit was tinkering with a strange contraption called a "gasoline buggy", in Baltimore the horse reigned supreme. The Horse Show was a regular event and society turned out in force for the judging of four-in-hands and other rigs.

Ottmar Mergenthaler (1854–1899)

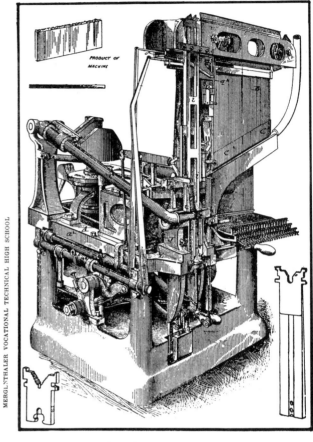

The first Linotype (1884)

The Linotype and the "Sub"

OTTMAR MERGENTHALER, a native German and watch repairer by trade, came to Baltimore in 1876 and set to work perfecting a machine for making slugs, each of which did the work of a line of hand-set type. His Linotype, patented in 1885, revolutionized printing. Baltimore newspapers, fearful of throwing printers out of their jobs, let New York have the honor of installing the first machine.

A few years later Simon Lake, Jersey husband of a Baltimore girl, began to build his submarine, the *Argonaut*, at Locust Point. In December, 1897, Lake took ten men and a woman on a thrilling hour's trip along the bottom of the harbor, from which, miraculously, they returned in safety.

The *Argonaut*, the first submarine with a combustion engine to make a successful cruise in deep water.

An unidentified Baltimore company

"Remember the Maine"

EARLY ON THE morning of February 16, 1898, Baltimoreans were awakened by newsboys crying "Extra" announcing the blowing up of the battleship *Maine*, with tragic loss of American lives. Instantly the battle cry "Remember the Maine" swept the country, and on April 25 Congress declared war against Spain.

To President McKinley's call for volunteers the young men of Baltimore made prompt response. Soon Pimlico was turned into a military camp with a city of tents inside the race track. There the public flocked in the afternoon to watch training and visit friends in uniform, while the pianos in row houses banged out "There'll Be a Hot Time in the Old Town Tonight". But as fighting started in grim earnest, public favor turned to the sad and sentimental "Goodby, Dolly Gray", "Break the News to Mother" and "As the Sun Went Down".

Baltimore units got no closer to the war than the southern states, but typhoid and dysentery took a heavier toll than Spanish bullets.

Spanish-American warriors at mess in the open

Pimlico as it looked on an afternoon in the Spring of 1898

Above, these smartly turned-out Baltimoreans are enjoying a dip at a popular seaside resort. No lady would appear on the beach without stockings. Right, "The Multigraph" was an ingenious way of showing a sitter from all angles. This charming young woman appears to be enjoying her own company.

BOTH PICTURES FROM THE MARYLAND HISTORICAL SOCIETY

Salute to the Gay Nineties

STEAMBOAT EXCURSIONS to Bay Ridge, Annapolis, Tolchester and Claiborne, the last connecting with trains to Ocean City. Week ends in Atlantic City and Cape May. Railway excursions daily on the Western Maryland to Pen-Mar for music, dancing, mountain drives and one of "Crout's Famous Pen-Mar Dinners (50c)"—Round-trip $1.00, Children 50c. De Wolfe Hopper starring in "El Capitan", featuring John Philip Sousa's stirring march, at the Academy of Music; a Blaney farce at the Holliday Street, and the "White Crook" burlesque company at Kernan's Monumental. Picnics at Gwynn Oak and Emory Grove and hurdy-gurdies grinding out the song hit "Just Tell Them that You Saw Me". These were some of the Baltimore diversions that made the Gay Nineties gay. Bicycles, too, were the rage.

ENOCH PRATT FREE LIBRARY

Here are a group of female bicyclists who have paused for a moment in their spin. Short skirts which revealed the ankles shocked the older generations, who asked what on earth the world was coming to.

Right, a typical interior of the Nineties. The house was on Auchentoroly Terrace. Note the bric-a-brac adorning the what-not and other evidences of the impeccable taste of the day.

Opposite, a group of picnickers about to enjoy an outing at Gwynn Oak Park.

85

1900-1925

A New Century
and a Millennium
That Went Astray

THE TWENTIETH CENTURY dawned upon an almost perfect world. In the few remote corners where heathen remained, missionaries were on the scene and laboring prodigiously. With the millennium just around the corner a spirit of tranquillity pervaded the air.

Baltimore shared this rosy outlook. The Federal census of 1900 gave the city a population of 508,938. Baltimore indignantly charged inaccuracy, made its own count, and raised the total to 517,035. The seventeen per cent increase over the previous decade was less than that in the new cities of the Middle West and in the industrial centers of the North, but it nevertheless indicated a healthy growth.

Food was plentiful; and, while incomes were low, so were prices. Theaters, amusement parks, athletic clubs and country clubs furnished entertainment, so that there was never a dull moment.

The century was only four years old when the city was visited by a disastrous fire. But the people of Baltimore—and particularly the businessmen on whose leadership the prosperity of the city depended —rose nobly to the occasion, and soon had erected a modern edifice on the foundations of the old.

In the flight of the Wright brothers at Kitty Hawk, N. C., and the rare automobiles seen on the streets in Baltimore, few discerned the instruments of a social revolution that was to turn things upside down in a matter of years. Nor did anybody dream that, during the first quarter of the new century, the whole civilized world would be plunged into a war of greater magnitude than any which had gone before. Never before in the city's history had there been so great a change in so short a time as in the period between 1900 and 1925.

Tranquillity was the keynote. Mount Vernon Place in 1900, looking west from St. Paul Street

Above, Bay steamers at Light Street. When this picture was taken there were as many more on their runs. Left, the Broadway-Locust Point Ferry. It ceased operations in 1939.

Right, two views of the oyster fleet. Their cargoes sold, oystermen had a big night in town. Today, oysters reach the city by truck.

A banana steamer unloads. By 1958 Baltimore had become the nation's third banana port, unloading 4,000,000 stems a year.

On the Waterfront

IN THE 1900's the inner harbor was constantly alive with a variety of craft. During the day, steamers jammed the Light Street piers, and, in the afternoon, set out down the Bay for their numerous destinations. Ships of the United Fruit Company's White Fleet tied up on Pratt Street, and disposed of their bananas direct to customers. On week ends, in the "R" months, the picturesque oyster boats crowded the Long Dock and found a ready market for their succulent cargoes. City buyers dealt with commission men or with the captains, and carted their purchases to hotels, restaurants and retail seafood establishments. Meanwhile, like a giant pendulum, the Broadway-Locust Point Ferry swung back and forth between its terminals. It saved many miles over the circuitous all-land route.

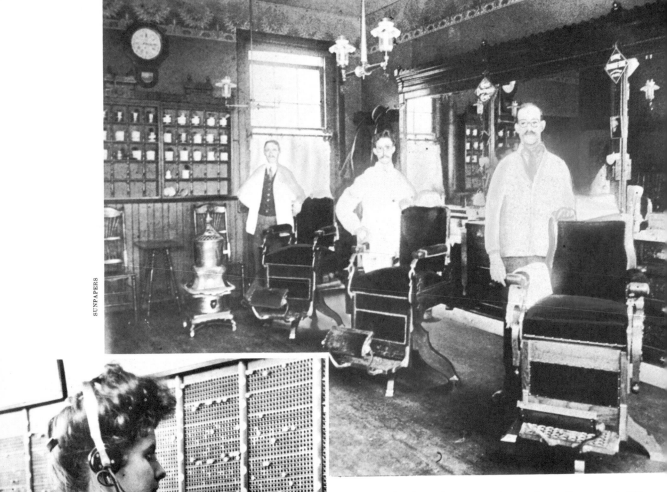

This barber shop was located at Paca and West Franklin Streets. At left, a fair employee of the Chesapeake & Potomac Telephone Company at the switchboard. Below, the first cable goes underground on Howard Street in 1901.

As the Century Began

A ROMANTIC FIGURE of the 1900's was the telephone girl, whose sweet voice inquired "Number, please?" when the receiver was lifted off the hook. With her pompadour and crocheted shirtwaist she was as fetching as her voice.

Haircuts in those days cost the exorbitant sum of fifteen cents and shaves a whole dime! But the red plush barber chairs, the individual shaving mugs, the gaslight illumination and other de luxe appointments more than justified the price.

A graphic illustration of progress was the gradual disappearance of electric wires, as the cables of the United Electric Light and Power Company went underground.

Era of Emancipation

ONE THING IS CERTAIN—the place of the Twentieth Century woman was not always in the home, as the pictures on this page illustrate. Dressed in her best bib and tucker, she lent tone to social gatherings. And she proved her versatility in other ways. We have noted that when women took to riding bicycles in the Nineties shocked observers asked "What next?" One answer, among others, was her introduction to the manly art of self defense as, for example, taught at Goucher. There, a sound mind in a sound body was the ideal sought.

A pause in the festivities as the ladies comply with the request to "Look pleasant." The banners and badges seem to indicate a patriotic meeting.

ENOCH PRATT FREE LIBRARY

ENOCH PRATT FREE LIBRARY

Shades of D'Artagnan! The Goucher Class of 1904 have a go at each other with the foils. The exercise was designed also to add grace and improve the posture.

In Monument Square the peanut vender and his customers created the only traffic problem

Above, these frock-coated, helmeted sergeants up-held the majesty of the law in the Northwest District. Below, in the days before modern plumbing the O.E.A. (Odorless Excavating Apparatus) performed an essential job. Ask Grandpa.

"Cheese It, the Cop!"

The Children's Playground Association has a festival in Patterson Park. This volunteer organization was the forerunner of the city's Bureau of Recreation

t the Pace Was Slow

And the hand-powered "White Wing" kept the streets tidy

POLICEMEN of the 1900's were built for endurance rather than speed. A fleet-footed youngster, warned that the cop was on his trail, and choosing to run for it, had a good chance of escape.

In his slow, deliberate movements the cop was typical of an age in which anything above eighteen miles an hour was looked upon as speeding. Picture a Baltimore with no morning or afternoon rush period worthy the name, when an automobile seen on the street was exceptional. Even the downtown section, though busy, enjoyed a serenity in marked contrast with the turmoil of today. It was broken only occasionally by a runaway horse dashing head-long and imperilling the lives of passersby until some hero seized the bridle. It was an age in which the term "stomach ulcers" was rarely, if ever, heard; and the only cases of nerves then current were popu-larly supposed to have been brought on by drinking too much coffee.

This service was made by Samuel Kirk & Son, which opened a shop on Market Street in 1815. Since colonial times Baltimore has been distinguished for its silversmiths

Do You Remember When — ?

ELDERLY BALTIMOREANS will readily recall the people, places and events pictured here. Who among them have not sometime thrilled to the "Dandy Fifth", in their dress uniforms of gray and gold, on parade; or, visiting Druid Hill Park, come on George (Mac) McLeary, with his dogs and staff, shepherding his flock of Southdowns?

Many Baltimoreans, no doubt, contributed to the complete dinner service presented in 1906 by the citizens of Maryland to the U.S. Cruiser *Maryland*. Each piece was decorated with scenes depicting local historic incidents.

The country road depicted below—believe it or not—is North Charles Street at 33rd, looking south. The picture was taken around 1903

COURTESY OF MR. H. FINDLAY FRENCH

94

The "Dandy Fifth" stands at ease on Mt. Royal Avenue, awaiting the order to march. The Lyric is in the background

Right, Eutaw Place, looking southeast, in its prime in 1903. Below, "Mac" and his sheep. The flock, introduced in 1879, was broken up in 1945 for lack of a shepherd.

EXTRA! **BALTIMORE MORNING HERALD** EXTRA

ESTABLISHED 1875—WHOLE NUMBER 9073   MONDAY, FEBRUARY 8, 1904.   PRICE ONE CENT.

HEART OF BALTIMORE WRECKED BY GREATEST FIRE IN CITY'S HISTORY

A THOUSAND BUILDINGS BURNED; LOSS OVER $75,000,000

DYNAMITE USED TO COMBAT FLAMES IN VAIN—ALL OF CHIEF SKYSCRAPERS DESTROYED

EXTRA ENGINES BROUGHT HERE FROM ALL THE NEIGHBORING CITIES

ENTIRE DISTRICT BETWEEN HOWARD AND GAY, FAYETTE AND PRATT STREETS IN RUINS

AT LIBERTY AND BALTIMORE STREETS.

ON HOPKINS PLACE.

ALONG LOMBARD STREET.

BLAKESLEE-LANE

Front page news—the morning after. When disaster struck, the Baltimore papers had to be published in Washington and Philadelphia

96

This picture was taken when the fire was at the height of its fury.

A City in Flames

THE WORST DISASTER in the history of Baltimore was the Great Fire of February 7, 1904. It was a raw, blustery Sunday, when at 10:45 A.M. an automatic alarm went off in the drygoods warehouse of John E. Hurst & Co., at German Street (now Redwood) and Hopkins Place. Whipped by the wind, the fire spread to near-by buildings and was quickly out of control, speeding north and east.

By mid-afternoon the whole of the city's fire department was battling the conflagration, but its puny streams of water were useless against the roaring sea of flame. Fire companies rushed by special train from New York, Philadelphia, Wilmington, Washington, York, and Hanover were no more effectual. Water failing, dynamite was used to blow up buildings to form a fire-break, but without success. As night came on the fire made a sight of terrifying grandeur, "fireproof" skyscrapers burning like giant torches. It halted only on reaching Jones Falls on Monday afternoon, leaving in its wake a vast expanse of smouldering ruins and a public too stunned fully to take in what had struck the city.

On the waterfront the fireboat *Cataract* is waging a hopeless battle against overwhelming odds.

97

Looking up Charles from Lombard — one sees O'Neill's on the left and the Union Trust on the right. To the left of City Hall are the B. & O. Building, the Equitable Building and the Calvert Building (then at Baltimore and Calvert Streets); to the right, the Maryland Trust and the Continental Trust.

The Phoenix Rises

THE FIRE was still burning when plans were set on foot to repair the damage. While the National Guard formed a cordon around the burned district to prevent looting, committees were organized to handle insurance claims, clean up the debris and lay out wider streets. Offers of financial help from outside were proudly refused. Indicative of the indomitable spirit of the local merchants, Baltimore newspapers the day after the fire were filled with the announcements of firms resuming business in temporary quarters. The total loss was estimated at from $100,000,000 to $150,000,000.

For weeks after the fire a popular Sunday afternoon diversion was a walk through the ruins, the high point being reached at the rusty remains of the fire engine that had been crushed by falling walls.

SUNPAPERS

SUNPAPERS

A map showing the burned district. The area covered 139.9 acres. A total of 1,343 buildings were destroyed, and 2,500 firms were temporarily put out of business.

Far left, police and guardsmen patrol the ruins. Center, Baltimore and Calvert Streets. Right, looking east from Baltimore and Charles Streets after the fire.

A friend takes these little patients from the Kernan Hospital for a spin. And what a thrill he gave them!

Right, Mr. Marburg is at the controls. Lower right, the cut-under runabout was especially designed for making sharp turns into narrow alleys and driveways.

They All Got There

THE EARLY 1900's were a period of transition from the horse-drawn vehicle to the automobile. The decade following Henry Ford's "horseless buggy" of 1893 saw many experiments from which evolved cars on the lavish scale of the one gracing this page. Still, many Baltimoreans stuck loyally by the horse.

There were mule teams in the city, too. The one shown here was purely imaginary. It adorned the menu for a dinner given at the Maryland Club in 1905, in honor of William A. Marburg, capitalist, by his Baltimore and New York friends.

The time is April, 1913. The Maryland Federation of Women's Clubs, 300 strong, just arrived from Washington, are off to McCoy Hall to hear a speech by Woodrow Wilson's daughter, Margaret.

The tollgate on Reisterstown Road is believed to have been the last one inside the city limits. It was abandoned in 1911.

Town and Country

HERE ARE THREE well-known localities as they looked a half century or so ago. The picture at the top of the page hardly needs to be identified as Mt. Royal Station. Nor, for that matter, do the ladies in the foreground. They are all clubwomen, of course, stylishly but sensibly dressed. But who would recognize the picture just above as the Reisterstown Road, south of Park Heights Avenue? The bottom picture, too, would keep many guessing. It is the Falls Road in 1906. Roland Park houses and the tennis courts of the Baltimore Country Club form the background.

Above, the *Antoinette* in flight. "Like a huge dragonfly", commented an observer. Left, an airship visits the shopping district.

Highflyers All

BALTIMOREANS had their first chance to see an airplane fly over the city on November 7, 1910, when Hubert Latham, pioneer French aviator, piloted his 50-h.p. monoplane, the *Antoinette*, over a twenty-two-mile course to win a $5,000 prize offered by *The Sunpapers*. The flight was made at an average height of 1,500 feet and speed of fifty miles an hour. Over 500,000 people crowded streets and roofs to witness this novel spectacle.

The year before, downtown Baltimore got a thrill when an airship, with one Fred Owens aboard, taking off from Electric Park, had to make a forced landing on a roof at Lexington and Liberty Streets.

The "highflyers" at the left did their flying on the ground. They illustrate what the best-dressed Baltimoreans were wearing about the time M. Latham came to town. The gentleman on the end refutes the saying, popular at the time, that if you saw a man in Baltimore walking with a cane he was either lame or an actor.

Great Surgeon —

Great Pupils

THIS RARE PHOTOGRAPH, made in 1904, shows Dr. William S. Halsted, first Professor of Surgery at the new Johns Hopkins Medical School and one of "the Four Doctors", performing an operation in the school's surgical amphitheater. Halsted was a perfectionist, of whom it was said his every operation was a work of art. Assisting him are a group of young doctors, then comparatively unknown, all of whom were destined to become outstanding in their special fields of surgery. Beginning with Dr. Halsted, and reading counter-clockwise around the operating table, are: Dr. Joseph C. Bloodgood, Dr. James F. Mitchell, Dr. J. M. T. Finney, Dr. Harvey Cushing, Helen H. Crawford, nurse; unidentified orderly, and Dr. Hugh H. Young.

JOHNS HOPKINS HOSPITAL

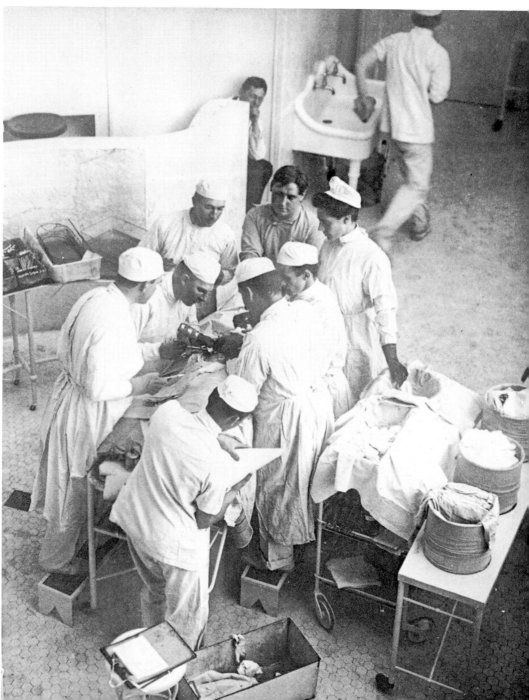

William Jennings Bryan (left) as he looked at the Convention

When They Nominated Woodrow Wilson

IN JUNE, 1912, Baltimore was turned topsy-turvy by the Democratic National Convention, meeting in the Fifth Regiment Armory. Hotels, boarding houses and other facilities were jammed with party leaders, delegates, newspaper men and other visitors.

Leading contenders for the presidential nomination were Champ Clark, Missouri Congressman, and Woodrow Wilson, Governor of New Jersey. William Jennings Bryan, the Great Commoner and veteran orator, held the balance of power.

When Bryan rose to speak, cheers for him were almost drowned out by catcalls and hisses, coming principally from the Tammany delegates. That was an old experience for Bryan who, nothing daunted, lashed out against the Wall Street reactionaries.

On the tenth ballot Clark had more than a majority, but the Democratic Convention observed the two-thirds rule. The tide was turned when Bryan delivered the Nebraska delegation to Wilson, who was nominated on the forty-sixth ballot.

The interior of the Fifth Regiment Armory during a meeting of the Convention.
Inset, a ticket needed to gain admission

A contemporary sketch showing Mt. Royal Station and the Armory. The
Armory's arched roof was destroyed during the fire of 1933

Joe Gans in fighting pose

When Babe was an Oriole. Seated by him is Jack Dunn, Jr. Standing, left to right, Manager Jack Dunn and Lefty Caporal

Augustus Schoenlein (Americus)

"Towers of Strength"

BALTIMORE in the 1900's was the home of three athletes who reached the heights in their respective sports. The oldest, Joe Gans, began his career as a prize fighter in 1894. In 1901 he became World's Lightweight Champion, a title he held until 1908. Old sports writers hailed him as the greatest fighter of all time.

Augustus J. Schoenlein, under the name of "Americus", wrestled when professional wrestling was an art and had not degenerated into "grunt and growl". He won the title of World's Light Heavyweight Champion in 1910.

Greatest of the three was the St. Mary's Industrial School boy, George Herman (Babe) Ruth. Babe joined the Baltimore club of the International Baseball League in 1914, was sold to the Boston Red Sox, and from there went on to fame and fortune with the New York Yankees.

Signal tower on Federal Hill

This tower, still standing in Patterson Park, is 60 feet tall

Just Towers

OF THE THREE towers shown here the most prominent is the Bromo-Seltzer Tower. When completed in 1911 it was the tallest building in town, rising 357 feet, and crowned with a giant revolving Bromo-Seltzer bottle.

Rhoda in her pagoda, "selling tea and syrup and soda", was the popular song hit around the time the pagoda-like observation tower was erected in Patterson Park in 1892.

The signal tower on Federal Hill replaced an earlier one that relayed news of approaching vessels. It stood there from 1887 to 1902.

The Bromo-Seltzer Tower is adapted from the Vecchio Palace tower in Florence, Italy. The bottle was taken down in 1936.

Stars of Stage and Screen

A PERENNIAL FAVORITE with Baltimore audiences of the 1900's was Texas-born Percy Haswell. In private life Mrs. George W. Fawcett, she starred in the stock company that bore her husband's name. In a single season at the fashionable Lyceum Theater, on North Charles Street, she displayed her versatility by essaying the leads in everything from "East Lynne" to Shakespeare.

At the height of his popularity Francis X. Bushman, pioneer screen lover, hardly dared dine at a public restaurant for fear of being mobbed by his admirers. Old Baltimore neighbors remembered him as the little boy who grew up on Argyle Avenue and "went for" Engine Company 13.

Percy Haswell made her debut in New York as Ada Rehan's understudy, then starred with William H. Crane before continuing her career in Baltimore

Not a winged Mercury, but Francis X. Bushman in his popular role as Messala in "Ben Hur"

A typical movie and its crew in the early days. "Admission, 5c". An important feature was the lady pianist who played throughout the reels, supplying pathos or humor, as the plot required.

A Movie, a Mart, and Twenty-Four Acres of Fun

Thousands of lights blazing at night gave Electric Park its name

An early Flower Mart. The cut of the tailored suits suggests that it may have been the earliest

A FAVORITE OBJECTIVE on a hot summer evening was Electric Park, covering twenty-four acres of land on Belvedere Avenue, near the Reisterstown Road. The park offered a variety of diversions, including a carousel, two roller coasters, a swimming pool, a boat lake, vaudeville, band concerts and a gripping cyclorama of the Johnstown Flood. Such joys are transient. The park was torn down in 1916.

To the Women's Civic League Baltimore owes its Flower Mart, which springs to life for one day each May, turning Mt. Vernon Place into a carnival. The first one was held in 1911.

109

A mushroom like that of an atomic bomb. This remarkable picture of the "Alum Chine" disaster was taken at a distance of two miles by Alfred Waldeck, a photographer who happened to be on the scene

The U.S. Frigate "Constellation" as she looked on her visit to Baltimore in 1914

"Alum Chine" and "Constellation"

DISASTER VISITED Baltimore on the morning of March 7, 1913, when the British freighter *Alum Chine*, lying off quarantine and loaded with dynamite for use in the construction of the Panama Canal, blew up. In the explosion and the fire which followed, thirty-three persons were killed and sixty injured. The blast shook the whole city and was felt as far away as Dover, Del.

A welcome sight in port the following year was the U.S. Frigate *Constellation*, which returned to her old home to take part in the Star-Spangled Banner Centennial. This historic vessel, which was designed by Joshua Humphreys and built by David Stodder on Harris Creek in the inner harbor, was launched on September 7, 1797.

> Doubt.
> Creeds grow so thick along
> the way,
> Their boughs hide God;
> I cannot pray.
>
> Lizette Woodworth Reese
>
> August 20, 1889.

Lizette Woodworth Reese

(1856-1935)

"SHE IS ONE of the imperishable glories of American letters, and she is the most distinguished woman who has ever lived in Baltimore." Such was H. L. Mencken's tribute to Lizette Woodworth Reese on her seventy-fifth birthday. For forty-five years a school teacher—twenty of them at Western High—Miss Reese published her first poem in 1874. She was best-known to the world for her sonnet "Tears", which appeared in 1909. In her autobiography, "A Victorian Village", she described her childhood in Waverly as only she could do it.

ALL PICTURES ON THIS PAGE FROM THE SUNPAPERS

TEARS

When I consider Life and its few years —
A wisp of fog betwixt us and the sun;
A call to battle, and the battle done
Ere the last echo dies within our ears;
A rose choked in the grass; an hour of fears;
The gusts that past a darkening shore do beat;
The burst of music down an unlistening street—
I wonder at the idleness of tears.
Ye old, old dead, and ye of yesternight,
Chieftains, and bards, and keepers of the sheep,
By every cup of sorrow that you had,
Loose me from tears, and make me see aright
How each hath back what once he stayed to weep;
Homer his sight, David his little lad!

Lizette Woodworth Reese

111

Above, the ruins of Mont-faucon, after the battle. Lower left, doughboys of the 115th man a trench in Alsace. Below, a field kitchen of the 313th.

Home at last! The 110th Field Artillery, composed mostly of Baltimore and Baltimore County men, disembarks at Newport News, Va.

"Lafayette, We Are Here"

THE POWERS of Western Europe had been at war for two and a half years when, in February, 1917, in the face of American protests, the Germans announced unrestricted submarine warfare. On April 6, the United States, already stung by the sinking of the *Lusitania* with heavy loss of American lives, declared a state of war existed with Germany.

Again Baltimoreans answered their country's call, serving on land, on sea and in the air. Among the combat units in General Pershing's American Expeditionary Force, in which Baltimore was heavily represented, were the 115th Infantry and the 110th Field Artillery, of the 29th Division, National Guard; and the 313th Infantry, 79th Division, National

Army. The 115th was a merger of the historic 5th, 4th and 1st Maryland Regiments.

By early summer the American forces had reached the battlefields of France. There were tense moments at home as news of the great allied Meuse-Argonne offensive was released. A brilliant action in that campaign was the capture of Montfaucon by the French and Americans. At a critical moment the 313th, proudly hailed as "Baltimore's Own", turned the tide by stemming a German counter-offensive.

Meanwhile fathers, mothers and sisters kept the home fires burning by buying Liberty Bonds, working in war industries, knitting socks and sweaters for the boys overseas, and tending the wounded.

113

Above, one of many cheering sections on the first Armistice Day. Left, a picture which needs no caption.

Sun Square as it looked at the height of the celebration.

Above, the 313th Infantry, "Baltimore's Own", passes in review on Mt. Vernon Place. Right, heading the parade of the 115th (at extreme left) is its commander, then Col. Milton A. Reckord.

"—It's Over, Over There!"

ON NOVEMBER 7, 1918, the news that an armistice had been signed was flashed over the cables and announced to the public, who greeted it with a delirium of joy. But the celebration was abruptly halted when a later dispatch stated that the first was false. Then, on November 11, came news of the real armistice. Baltimoreans once more thronged the streets, cheering, singing, dancing, waving flags, blowing horns and in every other conceivable way

marking the end of the dreadful suspense that had gripped the community from the time Maryland troops reached the front lines. There was sorrow only in those homes—fortunately few—where official notice had been received that a son had made the supreme sacrifice.

Then, in the early summer of 1919, Baltimore's patriotic emotions were again stirred by the return of the warriors themselves.

James Cardinal Gibbons (1834–1921) was loved and respected by persons of all faiths for his tolerance and his belief in American institutions. He is here seen at his last meeting with his good friend Theodore Roosevelt, at a victory loan rally in Baltimore in 1918

Three Faithful Stewards

HERE ARE PRESENTED three Baltimoreans—a man of God, a statesman and a philanthropist, each of whom made an impressive contribution to the world around him. James Gibbons was the second American to be appointed a cardinal of the Roman Catholic Church. Charles J. Bonaparte, grandson of Jerome and his American wife, Betsy Patterson, was a leading Maryland Republican who served as

Secretary of the Navy and Attorney-General in Theodore Roosevelt's cabinet. Henry Walters, in 1931, bequeathed to the city his art collection and several million dollars to maintain the gallery which bears the Walters name. In the thirty-seven years prior to his death he is reputed to have spent $1,000,000 a year adding to the collection left him by his father, William T. Walters.

Charles J. Bonaparte (1851–1921)

Henry Walters (1848–1931)

SUNPAPERS

Mt. Vernon Place, looking west, in 1923, during a statuary exhibit. The large mansion at the left, once Miss Mary Garrett's residence, was the first home of the Baltimore Museum of Art

PEALE MUSEUM

Old Lexington Market. Built on this site in 1803, it served, with minor alterations, as the city's source of choice foods for nearly 150 years

Shadow of a Pioneer City Planner

WERE JOHN EAGER HOWARD alive today, we may be sure he would be a leader in downtown redevelopment, as he was in the original development a century and a half ago. A landowner whose estate covered much of the heart of Baltimore and extended westward beyond Eutaw Street, he took an active interest in laying out that section of the city.

Among other donations, he gave the land for the Washington Monument, and for Lexington Market. He is said to have provided a site for the Roman Catholic Cathedral on terms so reasonable as virtually to constitute a benefaction. Here are two familiar landmarks, occupying sites once included in the Howard estate, as they looked in the 1920's.

117

HERE IS THE BUSY corner of Howard and Lexington Streets as it looked some forty years ago. Then as now, four of the city's largest department stores stood within a block of each other. Typical of the times was the "Traffic Cop", under his umbrella, operating the "Stop-Stop-Go-Go" signal by hand. While he directs the automobiles, another member of the force, selected for his gallantry, shepherds the lady shoppers across the street.

Now and then in the Spring, the district was enlivened by the blare and glamour of a circus parade. But even then it was known that the days of this fine American spectacle were numbered.

This picture was taken in the 1920's

Heart of the Shopping District

The parade is that of Ringling Brothers Circus on its visit to Baltimore in May, 1919

According to long-cherished custom, the mascots of the two service academies meet before the kickoff

This young woman wears the bathing suit that was smart in the middle 1920's. Note also the snappy two-piece affair on the gentleman in the background

The Navy Goat and the Army Mule

IN THE FALL OF 1924, Baltimore was the scene of that brilliant pageant and stellar athletic event— the Army-Navy football game. The weather was fine and the old stadium, by means of temporary stands, was stretched to hold a record crowd of 83,000 persons. The score—Army 12, Navy 0.

Summertime brought other diversions. A popular place to relax and cool off was the beach at Bay Shore. An extra attraction, not to be underestimated, were the bathing beauties, who exhibited their charms in one-piece bathing suits, then considered quite daring. But they still kept their stockings on.

BLAKESLEE-LANE

1925-1958

Meeting the Challenge

THE PERIOD of grace after World I was brief. With the rest of the country, Baltimore shared the heady exhilaration of the post-war boom and endured the tragic days of the Depression. The city made necessary adjustments to the New Deal, then stood up courageously under the sacrifices and heartaches of World War II.

As the first half of the century closed, peace was broken by hostilities in Korea; and, after that, the

sense of security was impaired by the cold war and the haunting threat of the atomic bomb.

The census of 1950 continued to show an increasing population inside the city limits. But it was in the adjacent counties that phenomenal growth had taken place. Metropolitan Baltimore's population now approached 1,500,000.

The prosperity of the city and its surrounding territory was revealed by a general taxable wealth esti-

The sky line of Baltimore in the early Forties, as seen from the ancient vantage point of Federal Hill

Changing World

mated at well over four billion dollars. Commerce and industry continued to present wide diversity. The port was still the city's greatest economic asset. Ship arrivals numbered around 6,000 a year, while total water-borne commerce approximated fifty million tons annually.

In spite of Hitler's growing shadow over Europe all was not gloom. These were the days when H. L. Mencken enlivened the local scene with his caustic wit, tilting at the Prohibitionists, chiding the "Booboisie" and taking outrageous liberties with the great and the near great. Among the highlights was a visit from young Charles Lindbergh, whose solo flight across the Atlantic marked a great step forward in the conquest of the air; and romance had its moment when the Duke and the Duchess of Windsor were tendered the freedom of the city.

Queen Marie and Mayor Howard W. Jackson on the way to the War Memorial, where the Queen appealed to American women to work for world peace

Mrs. Reuben Ross Holloway. She always wore a tall shako-like hat in her later years

"Sir Walter" Poultney, in characteristically gay attire, snapped on a visit to Atlantic City

Charles A. Lindbergh, just after stepping from the microphone at the old Stadium, where he addressed a crowd of 30,000. Beside him are Mayor William F. Broening and, to the rear, Governor Albert C. Ritchie.

Lindbergh Day

EAST SIDE — ENTER GATE 3 SECTION C

Celebration in honor of, and to commemorate

THE VISIT OF

Col. Charles A. Lindbergh

TO THE CITY OF BALTIMORE

Tuesday Afternoon, October 18, 1927

in the BALTIMORE STADIUM

WILLIAM I. NORRIS
President, Park Board

WILLIAM F. BROENING
Mayor of Baltimore

Right Royal Personages

ON NOVEMBER 20, 1926, Baltimore had the privilege of entertaining a queen in the person of the colorful Marie of Rumania. She was accompanied on her American tour by her children, Princess Ileana and Prince Nicholas. In spite of chilling rain and wind thousands turned out to see the royal party.

In October, 1927, another visitor to Baltimore received a royal welcome—boyish young Charles A. Lindbergh. A few months before, he had astonished the world by making a non-stop flight from New York to Paris, alone in his monoplane "The Spirit of St. Louis".

A familiar figure on Charles Street in those days was Walter de Curzon Poultney, Baltimore's Beau Brummel, who, because of his courtly manner, was dubbed "Sir Walter" by his friends. His cravats, shirts, gloves, spats and socks were of the liveliest colors. On one of his 38 trips to Europe he returned with a complete Tyrolean costume. He is said frequently to have changed his attire three times a day.

Beloved of all who knew her was Mrs. Reuben Ross Holloway, who identified herself as "a citizen and a patriot". Woe to anybody who, to her knowledge, showed disrespect to the Flag. For many years she waged a campaign to make "The Star-Spangled Banner" the National Anthem. Her zeal was rewarded when, on March 3, 1931, Congress passed the necessary legislation.

123

The Mail Line's flag-ship *City of Baltimore* on her first sailing, July 2, 1931. Round-trip fare was $180. Mail diffi-culties and European politics resulted in the line's suspension in the year 1938.

"All Ashore That's Going Ashore"

THROUGH THE YEARS, that familiar warning has been heard on passenger ships sailing out of Baltimore. Among these were the boats of the Old Bay Line, the Merchants and Miners, and the Baltimore Mail Line.

The Old Bay Line (Baltimore Steam Packet Com-pany), founded in 1840, maintained daily sailings to Norfolk up to December 30, 1959. The M. & M. (Merchants and Miners Transportation Company) was established in 1852 to carry leather from Balti-more tanneries to Boston's shoe factories. A voyage on one of those sturdy sea-going vessels was as good as a trip abroad. The line was dissolved in 1952, twenty-four days short of a century of operations. The Mail Line (Baltimore Mail Steamship Company) was a noble effort to restore overseas passenger and freight service with weekly sailings to Le Havre and Hamburg.

Above, the Old Bay Line's *State of Virginia.* Left, the M. & M's *Dorchester*, torpedoed in the North Atlantic on February 3, 1943, with the heroic "Four Chaplains" among those lost.

Right, Mildred Nat-wick and a "juvenile heavy", in a tense scene from a Vaga-bond production in 1932. In the inset be-low, Mildred Dunnock.

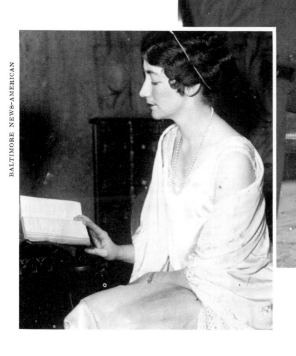

From Baltimore to Broadway

THE VAGABONDS staged their first performance on November 16, 1916. This enterprising amateur theatrical group now looks back over more than fifty years of activity, claiming to be America's oldest little theater still in operation. Conspicuous among its members who graduated to the professional stage are Mildred Natwick and Mildred Dunnock, products respectively of Bryn Mawr School and Goucher College. The two Mildreds are among Baltimore's best-known contributions to Broadway; both have starred also on the screen and in television.

John Charles Thomas's fine baritone voice carried him from a Peabody Conservatory scholarship to the Royal Opera (Brussels) and to the Metropolitan (New York). He appeared as well in musical comedy, on concert tours, and with the Philadelphia Grand Opera and the Baltimore Civic Opera.

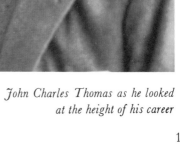

John Charles Thomas as he looked at the height of his career

Famous among point-to-point champions was Howard Bruce's Billy Barton (No. 8) who, ridden by Albert G. Ober, Jr., in 1926 won the Maryland Grand National, the Maryland Hunt Cup and the Virginia Gold Cup. Entered in England's great steeplechase at Aintree in 1928, Billy ran a fine race but fell at the last fence

Test for a Champion

ON THREE SUCCESSIVE Saturdays in each April Baltimoreans flock to the hunting country north of the city to witness the spectacular point-to-point races. The third and crowning event is the Maryland Hunt Cup, first run in 1894. The race is now held in Worthington Valley over a four-mile course, with twenty-two jumps, varying in height from two feet four inches to five feet. This is strictly an amateur event; all the winner gets is a cup—and glory. Following the death of a valuable horse and a succession of accidents to riders, a local sportsman was asked why the course was not made easier in order to reduce the hazard. "There can be but one champion", was his uncompromising reply.

A thrilling moment in the Hunt Cup. A rider meets with disaster early in the race

The Easter Parade in 1931

Above, the organ-grinder and his monkey amuse young and old. Right: Yes, Baltimore had its "El". It was built over Guilford Avenue, from Lexington to Biddle. Erected in 1892, it was torn down in 1950.

Springtime in Baltimore in the 30's

TRADITIONALLY Spring is counted in Baltimore from the time the first crocus shows its head in the Archbishop's garden. A few weeks later comes Easter Sunday, with its church services in the morning, and in the afternoon, the Charles Street Easter Parade. By 1930 the dominance of the automobile had shifted the scene of the parade, now turned into a "motorcade", northward to the segment of Charles Street between 28th and University Parkway.

Springtime in Baltimore, in the early 30's as today, was magnolias bursting into bloom below Lafayette's statue, tulips in Preston Gardens, and young couples unashamedly holding hands as they strolled on streets bathed in sunshine. It was a balmy atmosphere that seemed to say, "Why hurry, when there is so much here to enjoy?"

H. L. Mencken —
Editor, Author,
Critic, Scholar

(1880–1956)

Mencken in 1936

BORN IN BALTIMORE in 1880, Henry Louis Mencken began his literary career as a reporter on the old *Morning Herald*, later becoming editor of *The Evening Herald*. After the demise of those newspapers, he moved to the editorial staffs of *The Sun* and *The Evening Sun*.

It was as a critic of the American scene that he achieved national distinction. With a biting wit and a genius for ridicule he waged war against complacency, hypocrisy and cant, and raised such a storm that one of his biographers has called him "Disturber of the Peace".

But Mencken was not always doing battle. A man of high good humor, he loved the company of inti-mate friends. Nowhere was that trait more fully displayed than in his activities with the Saturday Night Club. This was a group of a dozen or so men who met weekly to pool their musical talents, and then gather around a table for refreshments and conviviality. In the impromptu orchestra, which always included a symphony on its program, Mencken played the piano. He began lessons at the age of eight.

His treatise, *The American Language*, is a serious, scholarly work that assures him a permanent place among the philologists. Much of his writing was done in the quiet of his almost lifelong home on Hollins Street, where he enjoyed the respect and affection of his neighbors.

The Saturday Night Club about to go into action. Top right, the club's official coat-of-arms. Right, the study at 1524 Hollins Street, where Mencken did his work.

"Pretty good. Not bad at all." Thus Mencken, with friends at the Rennert bar, greeted the return of 3.2 per cent beer, at 12.01 A.M., April 7, 1933.

Hopkins Olympic Team, 1932, in the stadium at Los Angeles

Right, Navy-Notre Dame football game, October, 1935, in the old Stadium. The attendance was 60,000.

World Champions and a Gridiron Classic

LIVING UP to its reputation for turning out fine lacrosse teams, the Johns Hopkins University won the honor of representing the United States at the Olympic Games at the Hague in 1928, and again at Los Angeles in 1932. In both instances the teams came home world champions. The team of 1932 had an unblemished record. Having won all its games in the regular season, it went on to defeat the Canadians at Los Angeles for the championship, two out of three.

In the 1930's the most popular amateur football games played in Baltimore were those between Navy and Notre Dame. The teams were well-matched and rivalry between the Middies and the Fighting Irish keen. Fair weather or foul, a record crowd was always on hand and seldom was it disappointed. Among college games in the East, Navy-Notre Dame continues to be a stellar event in the gridiron season.

The Duke and Duchess of Windsor mount the steps of the City Hall to receive the official welcome of the municipality. Through cheering crowds the Windsors then made a royal progress to the Baltimore Country Club.

Below is Seabiscuit romping home, setting a track record of 1.56⅗ for the mile and three-sixteenths course.

" . . . the Woman I Love "

THE BRITISH EMPIRE was shaken to its foundations when, in a memorable broadcast on December 10, 1936, King Edward VIII announced his abdication for ". . . the woman I love". A highlight of pre-World War II days in Baltimore was the official visit of the Duke and Duchess of Windsor, on October 13, 1941. Then Baltimore had an opportunity to welcome home her own daughter, the former Wallis Warfield, for whose love a king had sacrificed his throne.

Another highlight of the pre-war era was the meeting at Pimlico, on November 1, 1938, between Mr. C. S. Howard's Seabiscuit and Mr. Samuel Riddle's War Admiral, before a crowd of 40,000 people. Sportsmen called it one of the greatest match races in the history of the American turf. Seabiscuit won by four lengths.

BALTIMORE NEWS-AMERICAN

The *Patrick Henry*, first Liberty ship to be launched in the nation, and one of the 384 Liberty ships built at the Bethlehem-Fairfield shipyards, whose 47,000 workers also built 94 Victory ships and 30 LST's. Baltimore shipyards completed a total of 608 ships, and repaired thousands more. Above, Howard Street in war time with a detachment of "Gobs" on the way to a new station.

World War II — Abroad and at Home

This Martin Mars, the largest flying boat built in the country, was the first of several constructed at the Glenn L. Martin plant for the U. S. Navy. She saw seventeen months' service flying cargoes across the Pacific. The weight of this so-called "Flying Liberty Ship" was 77 tons

Above, a filter center unit plots airplane movements. Right, Red Cross
volunteers provide between-train coffee
and buns for service men. Below, typical war workers.

BALTIMORE CHAPTER, AMERICAN RED CROSS

SUNPAPERS

EVEN BEFORE Pearl Harbor many Baltimoreans were
in uniform. As the war progressed thousands more
saw service with the nation's armed forces in all parts
of the world. Baltimoreans were among the winners
of the Congressional Medal of Honor and of other
awards for heroism; and, in distant battlefield
cemeteries, many a Cross or Star of David marked the
last resting place of a son who was not to return.

At home Baltimore's factories and shipyards were
contributing their share to the greatest war production effort the world had ever known. Persons not
engaged in the war industries, while struggling with
rationing cards, volunteered for Red Cross work, for
service on draft and rationing boards, or for jobs in
civilian defense in anticipation of an air raid which,
fortunately, never came.

*This was the scene that greeted men of the 29th Division as they landed on Omaha Beach.
In this operation the division lost 500 men, killed or wounded*

*The hedgerows of Normandy as seen from the air.
It was through such difficult country as this that men
who survived the landing had to fight their way*

From Omaha Beach
to Victory

BALTIMORE'S STAKE in the Normandy landing was large. For in the vanguard of the forces wading ashore on Omaha Beach, in the gray dawn of June 6, 1944, was the 29th Division, originally composed in part of Maryland National Guard units. Still in the division were many Baltimoreans. And there were Baltimoreans too in other divisions of the Allied armies. So it was with tense feelings that the people at home watched the fighting in Europe, from the Normandy hedgerows to the invasion of Germany.

Then came V-E Day, with unconditional surrender, relief from prolonged suspense, and public rejoicing such as attended Armistice Day, 1918. Four months later followed V-J Day, and the gradual home-coming of the armed forces from all the theaters of war to the peace and serenity of civilian life.

Sun Square on V-E Day, May 7, 1945. The smiles on the faces of these young people illustrate the relief felt throughout the city.

An impressive post-war visitor. The U.S. aircraft carrier "Randolph" passes the guns of Fort McHenry on her way up the harbor to celebrate Navy Week in October, 1945

MAPS, INCORPORATED

BALTIMORE NEWS-AMERICAN

Above, Friendship Airport. Left, President Truman, with Governor William Preston Lane of Maryland on his right, and Mayor Thomas D'Alesandro, Jr. of Baltimore on his left.

Max Hochschild on his 100th birthday

A New Airport and An Old Baltimorean

HERE IS PRESENTED a contrast in ages—an airport in its infancy, and a venerable citizen whose life almost spanned the century pictured in this volume.

On June 25, 1950, Friendship International Airport, south of the city in Anne Arundel County, was dedicated by President Harry S Truman. Its total cost was $15,000,000, of which the people of Baltimore contributed no less than $12,000,000.

Born in Gross Rohrheim, Germany, on June 14, 1855, Max Hochschild in his youth emigrated to the United States, and made his home in Baltimore. He was one of the founders in 1897 of the store that bears his name, and at the age of 101 took part, along with his great-grandson, Jimmy Hutzler, in the opening ceremonies at the Eastpoint Shopping Center in 1956. Mr. Hochschild died on June 1, 1957.

These lions couchant once guarded Guilford, the country home of A. S. Abell, the publisher. They now perform the same duty at the residence of a member of the Abell family at 5501 Roland Avenue

A Pride of Lions

LIKE VENICE, Baltimore boasts lions of distinction. Here are a few of the conspicuous examples.

Foremost among the local breed are, of course, the four stone lions that for so many years adorned the old Calvert Street Bridge. The story goes that on a winter's evening in 1880, Larry Finnegan, Eighth Ward Irishman, by way of defying the British, twisted off the lions' tails. Replacing the stone tails with bronze tails cost the municipality $110. Now that the old bridge is no more, the lions, appropriately enough, have been given a new home at the Druid Hill Park Zoo.

This ferocious beast and his mate greet visitors to the Baltimore Museum of Art

A Calvert Street Bridge lion, bronze tail and all

In 1950, King and Queen were real lions at the Zoo

Dignity personified. The Barye lion in Mt. Vernon Place

Charles Street looking north. The tall buildings on the left are Charles Center. To the right the graceful tower of the Maryland National Bank building still dominates.

Battle for Survival, and Rebirth

THE PAST TEN YEARS witnessed throughout the nation the impact of two dynamic forces; namely, continued rapid growth of population, and the flight from the city to the suburbs. Baltimore felt keenly the effect of both. While the population in the metropolitan district grew by leaps and bounds, that of the inner city declined. To magnify the problem, the more affluent citizens moved out and left the masses of the underprivileged behind. The result was severe economic loss to the inner city. Property values took a downward plunge, business suffered and once prosperous neighborhoods degenerated into slums.

The impelling question was how to reverse the trend. The solution called for bold and intelligent planning. The leaders in the community proved equal to the task. Acting through volunteer organizations, obtaining the approval of Mayor and City Council and enlisting aid from the Federal Government, they initiated a program of construction and rehabilitation which has altered the face of the city. Along with this went a vast expansion in education, the arts, recreation, business, industry, transportation and communications. Much remains to be done. Today's skyline, viewed from four directions, tells part of the story.

Approach to the city from the southwest. In the foreground is the Russell Street viaduct.

Above, looking west from Broadway. This picture was taken from the roof of the Johns Hopkins Hospital.

*Below, looking southeast from Sutton Place. Familiar landmarks, such as the spire of the
First Presbyterian Church, identify this as still being Baltimore.*

A birdseye view of Charles Center. It is bounded by Charles, Saratoga and Lombard Streets, Hopkins Place and Liberty Street. At right, the Center at night looking east. The high-rise office buildings in the foreground are One Charles Center and the Blaustein Building; the latter not in, but adjacent to, the Center.

The Miracle that is Charles Center

SKEPTICS SAID it couldn't be done; at least not in Baltimore. Back in 1958 incredulity greeted the joint proposal of the Committee for Downtown and the Greater Baltimore Committee to level 33 acres in the heart of the city and replace the tired old structures with modern office buildings, high-rise apartments, two theaters, a hotel, retail shops, underground parking, and parks, at an estimated cost of $130,000,000.

Notwithstanding, a Master Plan, financed by the committees, was approved by the City, and the public voted a bond issue. Ground was broken in August, 1961. Thus was Charles Center born. By 1968 eighty-five per cent of it was complete.

Above, Hopkins Place. An inviting spot in fine weather, especially to office workers at the noon hour. In the foreground is the Morris A. Mechanic Theater; and across Baltimore Street, the Lord Baltimore Hotel and the B. & O. Building. At far right, the Maryland National Bank Building.

At left, a panorama of the Center looking toward the Southeast, showing the 23-story Statler-Hilton Hotel, and beyond it the Blaustein Building, the Vermont Federal Building, the Lord Baltimore Hotel, the Sun Life, and the massive Federal Building.

141

Above, the $14,000,000 Civic Center, opposite Charles Center. With 12,420 seats and 100,000 square feet of floor space, it serves for basketball, hockey, track meets, ice shows, concerts, conventions; and even the circus.

At right, Charles Center, looking north. The upper level walkway over Baltimore Street is to relieve pedestrians of traffic hazards.

Above, architects' renderings of the two Tower Apartments, nearing completion, and the $16,000,000 Mercantile, Safe Deposit and Trust Company Building, soon to rise. The Towers, respectively 27 and 30 stories high, provide 400 apartments.

At left, the Gas & Electric Company Building's new annex, as seen from the plaza between One Charles Center and the Fidelity & Deposit Building on Charles Street.

143

The central building of the Enoch Pratt Free Library, on Cathedral Street between Franklin and Mulberry, was completed in 1933. Note the twelve large show windows in the front.

Museums, a Library and a Treasury of Local History

BALTIMORE's public institutions provide abundant material for the student, the connoisseur and the sightseer. The Peale (Municipal) Museum, the first City Hall of Baltimore, and the Peabody Library are illustrated on earlier pages. The Baltimore Museum of Art and the Walters Art Gallery together contain notable collections, from the days of the Pharaohs to the moderns. The Pratt Library, with its many branches throughout the city, is an unending source of learning and enjoyment. The Maryland Historical Society serves the community and the nation in preserving the Free State heritage. For those whose hobby is railroads the B. & O.'s Transportation Museum is a rare delight. The Flag House is the only building in the United States privileged by Act of Congress to fly, day and night, both the National Flag and the Star-Spangled Banner of 1814.

The Maryland Historical Society, on West Monument Street. In the foreground is the new Thomas and Hugg Memorial Wing, completed in 1967; and, left, the Keyser Memorial Building, formerly the home of Enoch Pratt. In the latter is one of the Society's treasures—Francis Scott Key's original manuscript of "The Star-Spangled Banner."

144

MARION E. WARREN

BALTIMORE MUSEUM OF ART

WALTERS ART GALLERY

Above, the Baltimore Museum of Art, in Wyman Park. At left, a special exhibit of photographs of sports which drew large crowds.

Below, the Flag House at 844 East Pratt Street, where Mary Pickersgill made the original Star Spangled Banner; size 30 by 42 feet.

Above, the main court of the Walters Art Gallery. It is used for classical exhibits. The building was opened in 1909. Below, an ancient locomotive and cars in the B. & O. Museum, which is a paradise for railroad buffs.

MARION E. WARREN

SUNPAPERS

145

At right, a demonstration of the "Barnes Dance." Pedestrians enjoy the right of way while motorists wait.

Above, Traffic Director Barnes, against a background of "No Parking" signs that Baltimoreans learned to respect.

At right, a section of Baltimore's Beltway showing the Route 40 cloverleaf. This modern highway circling the city measures 32.1 miles.

Baltimore's Traffic Problem and the Barnes Era

MODERN TRAFFIC REGULATION may be said to have begun in Baltimore when, in 1953, Henry A. Barnes took over as Traffic Director. Baltimoreans who until then had parked their cars almost when and where they pleased, were shocked to find that the new hand, indifferent to prevailing custom, felt no compunction about hauling away those cars that violated his rules. He was quite as ruthless in decreeing one-way streets to enlarge the traffic arteries. But protests ended when the populace observed the results. Associated with his regime were the "Barnes Dance", giving pedestrians right of way at intersections, and a computer control system, sometimes called the "Barnes Brain". After Mr. Barnes moved to New York, progress continued in the handling of the fast growing numbers of cars. The Harbor Tunnel had been opened in 1957. In the 1960's came the Baltimore Beltway and the expressways that have revolutionized traffic movement in and around the city. The East-West Expressway, whose city route has long been a bone of contention, is still in the future.

Above, the Harbor Tunnel lies under the Patapsco River, between Fairfield and Canton. The picture shows the Fairfield entrance. The tunnel cost $130,000,000.

Above, the Traffic Control and Communication Center. Here information picked up by radar stations is fed into computers which automatically regulate traffic lights throughout the city.

At right, this intricate pattern is fashioned by the 28th Street Interchange on the Jones Falls Expressway, opened from downtown to Beltway in 1962.

"They're Off!" Or are they? The thoroughbreds in the Hopkins Medical School's Turtle Derby are sometimes reluctant to start. The contest bears out the Old Testament's reminder that the race is not always to the swift.

Well, here they are. The white marble steps which have long been a part of the local tradition.

At left, the Flower Mart, sponsored by the Women's Civic League. First held in 1911 it has missed only one year, during World War II, and maintains its popularity.

MARYLAND JOCKEY CLUB

PREAKNESS 1966

MARION E. WARREN

Above, the field rounds the turn in the running of the Preakness. This gruelling contest, run over a course of a mile and three-sixteenths, shares honors with the two other classics for three-year olds—the Kentucky Derby and the Belmont.

At left, a winner receives congratulations. Since it is too early in the season for "Susans", the black-eyes have to be painted in.

Below, a corner of the Sherwood Gardens showing the profusion of tulips and azaleas.

A. AUBREY BODINE

Baltimore in the Merry Month of May

IT IS THE MONTH of the Flower Mart in Mount Vernon Place. It is the month of the House and Garden Pilgrimage, when many of the finest houses and gardens in the city and the various counties are open to the public. It is the month when the Sherwood Gardens, in Guilford, reach their peak and attract thousands of visitors. It is the month when many more thousands—racing enthusiasts from all parts of the country—journey to "Old Hilltop" to see the running of the Preakness, classic for three-year olds. The race over, the winner returns for weighing-in and gets a blanket of "Black-eyed Susans", Maryland's official flower. It is the month of the merriest of all sporting jests, the Johns Hopkins Medical School's "Turtle Derby."

GREATER BALTIMORE MEDICAL CENTER

A birdseye view of the Greater Baltimore Medical Center, situated on a lofty hill off Charles Street Avenue. Towson is seen in the distance. "GBMC" arose from a merger of the Hospital for the Women of Maryland and the Presbyterian Eye, Ear and Throat Hospital. Erected at a cost of $14,000,000, it was dedicated in 1965.

A. AUBREY BODINE

Above, Sinai Hospital which moved from east Baltimore to the northwest suburbs in 1959. It cost $20,000,000 and provides 480 beds.

Below, the $8,000,000 Mercy Hospital, opened in 1963. Mercy elected to stay in town. The finishing of 4 top floors is adding 80 beds.

Hospitals Expand to Meet Growing Needs

MODERN MEDICAL CARE, involving specialists and costly equipment, is centered on the hospital. That, added to population growth, has required major expansion in hospital facilities. Since 1958, completed or planned construction in the Baltimore area by the voluntary hospitals, exclusive of government institutions, is estimated to represent a total outlay of $202,000,000. More than 1000 beds have been added, with over 700 new ones in immediate prospect, and not including expansion still a few years off. While the tendency has been for hospitals to seek broader space in the suburbs, several have elected to remain in the city, the better to serve that area. Some sixteen voluntary hospitals have shared in this growth.

A. AUBREY BODINE

St. Joseph, at a cost of $12,500,000, provides 342 beds. It is on 23 acres adjoining "GBMC."

St. Agnes Hospital, its capacity increased to 396 beds, lies in southwest Baltimore.

Wing of Church Home and Hospital, erected in 1958, provides 200 patient beds and homes for 39 ladies. Still another building is going up.

151

Above, a supermarket. Above at right, an audience enjoys a concert in a major shopping center plaza.

Typical of the modern department store are goods artfully displayed; and, of course, escalators.

Essential to the job is the ubiquitous shopping cart.

In America Everybody "Goes to the Store"

ENGLAND has been called "a nation of shopkeepers." America today might well be called "a nation of shoppers." Downtown stores still attract many customers, but an outstanding feature of late years has been the rise of the shopping center. There is at least one in every suburban area, where supermarkets and a variety of retail stores offer goods and services to meet every need, while neighborhood movies provide entertainment. Nor is it unusual for a center to stage a play or concert.

Above, at left, a rehearsal on Center Stage. At right, a scene from "Hello, Dolly" which opened the Mechanic.

At left, spacious interior of the Mechanic Theater. It seats 1805. Subscription list is over 20,000.

Below, the versatile Civic Center accommodates the Barnum and Bailey-Ringling Brothers Circus.

The Theater World Takes on New Life

THE MOST IMPORTANT event in the past decade in the Baltimore theatrical world has been the construction of the magnificent Morris A. Mechanic Theater, in Charles Center. It has been steadily booked with important Broadway shows since its opening on January 16, 1967. Other playhouses are Center Stage, with a residential professional company; Painters Mill, specializing in musicals; and Oregon Ridge, where patrons dine before the show. Then there is the Civic Center.

MARION E. WARREN

Above, the Baltimore Symphony Orchestra, under the baton of Peter Herman Adler, as it looks to the audience in the course of a concert at the Lyric Theater.

At left, Rosa Ponselle, Metropolitan star who sang with Caruso, sometimes called "First Lady of Opera." She is artistic director and guiding spirit of the local company.

Symphony, Grand Opera and Ballet

154

Star soloists are brought in for large scale performances of the ballet, which is capable of productions with as many as sixty dancers.

A scene from La Traviata *by the Civic Opera. In its eighteen-year history its repertoire has included some 26 operas.*

BALTIMORE is well represented in these three major performing arts. Oldest of the organizations is the Symphony Orchestra whose first program was presented on February 11, 1916. In a normal season it gives 24 mid-week and 12 Saturday night concerts, and tours Maryland counties and some half dozen states.

The Baltimore Civic Opera Company was incorporated as a non-profit organization in 1950. In the succeeding years, accompanied by the symphony orchestra, a high degree of excellence in music and staging has been attained. Performances have increased from six to nine in the season series. Support has come from a Ford Foundation grant, local contributions and the sale of tickets. The Opera has never approached City, State or Federal Government for help.

Youngest of the trio is the Baltimore City Ballet Company, founded in 1961. Since then it has given well over 100 performances. Full-time dancers on salaries are augmented by a local company of apprentices and students.

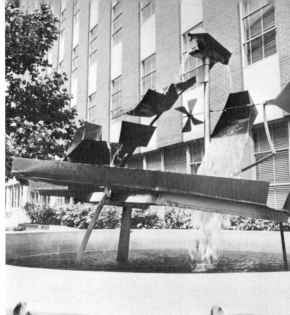

The Jacob France Fountain in Charles Center is "a thing of beauty"; and, let us hope "a joy forever."

This ingenious illustration of cause and effect graces 707 North Calvert Street.

The fountain in Courthouse Square. An ideal spot for "girl watching."

This geyser-like fountain and reflecting pool adorn the State Roads Commission Building in Mount Royal Plaza.

Fountains Stage a Comeback

WHILE THE FOUNTAINS of Baltimore are not as famous as those of Rome they have had an honorable place in local history and legend. Witness those in Mount Vernon Place, where a young lady and her escort scandalized society in Victorian days by wading through in evening clothes, and where today the tossing of a penny will make a wish come true. And there were the gorgeous fountains on Eutaw Place at the turn of the century. Then came a time when they seemed to go out of style. Many of the old ones deteriorated and no new ones were added. But of late fountains have enjoyed a revival. The pictures on this page illustrate how they are being used to beautify the city of today. And who would deny that they do it nicely?

The Little Leaguer soon learns the first rudiment of baseball; that is, razzing the umpire.

Amateur Sports— from Jousting to Motor-Boating

IN THE FIELD of amateur sports Baltimoreans are participants as well as spectators. Football, baseball, basketball, track, wrestling and lacrosse begin in high school and continue through college. The tidewaters of the Patapsco and the Bay and upland rivers offer unexcelled opportunity for boating and fishing. Sailing is as old as the Bay itself; and, of late years, the local public has joined in the national craze for power boats, from outboard motors to deluxe yachts.

In the Baltimore area the horse is far from dead. Witness the fox hunting, the point-to-point racing and the riding schools. Believe it or not, medieval jousting is Maryland's official sport. The pictures on this page provide only a sampling.

Water sports a la carte. A family party enjoys a motorboat outing, while another motorboat approaches. Note the sailboats in the distance.

Above, the ancient sport of jousting. The object is to get the lance through the ring while riding at a gallop.

Below, Baltimore is the home of lacrosse. Old rivals, Johns Hopkins University and the Mount Washington Club, battle it out at Homewood.

The World Championship Team of 1966. They could afford to smile.

Above, part of the sell-out crowd of more than 50,000 who saw the game.

At right, Dave McNally gives a shout of triumph as Brooks Robinson leaps in the air.

Champions Again
After Seventy Years

THE ORIOLES had not held the World Championship since 1896. Then in 1966 they won the title again. It had been a long wait, but when it came what a victory it was! Four straight over the Los Angeles Dodgers, of the National League, who were rated the favorite. The series closed dramatically on Sunday, October 10, when, at Memorial Stadium before a crowd of 54,458, Dave McNally pitched a brilliant 1–0 shutout, and Frank Robinson sewed it up for the Birds with a 410-foot drive into the left field stands.

158

At right, Paul Blair makes the catch that ended it.

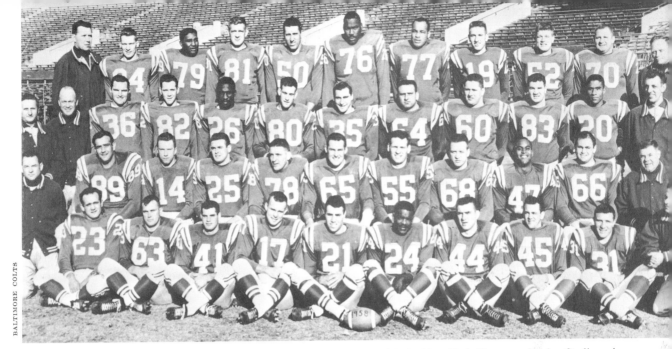

The championship team of 1958. The "sudden death" extra period game with the New York Giants, at Yankee Stadium, in which the Colts won the title, 23–17, has been called the greatest football game in history.

Above, Alan Ameche breaks through for the winning touchdown.

At right, John Unitas, No. 19, gets off one of his famous passes.

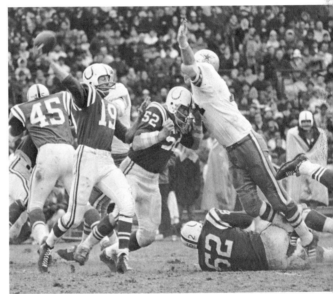

The Colts "Came, Saw, and Conquered"

THE COLTS have represented Baltimore in the National Football League since 1953. During their 14-year career they have won two world championships (1958 and 1959) and one division championship (1964). The home games at Memorial Stadium on Sunday afternoons during the fall and early winter attract sell-out crowds of hardy fans who are not afraid of the often frigid temperature. There is much entertaining before and after the games, and the holders of season tickets enjoy rare prestige in the community.

At left, The Stadium is always filled to capacity, 60,238.

159

At left, it looks like a sure basket. The Bullets, of the National Basketball Association, in action in the Civic Center.

Below, a rough moment in a Clipper hockey match. Speed, skill and fight give this sport its popular appeal.

At right, the Bays at Memorial Stadium. Until American players are developed, "pro" soccer teams must depend on men from other countries.

Clippers, Bullets and Bays

TIME WAS when sports writers took a rest between the football and the baseball seasons, but no longer. Basketball and ice hockey have seized the public imagination and filled the gap. The Civic Center, whose playing space can be readily changed from ice rink to floor, made both sports possible locally on a big league basis. The Clippers, with an American League franchise, were the first Civic Center tenants. The Bullets, of the National Basketball League, followed.

In 1967 the Baltimore Bays became a charter member of the new National Professional Soccer League. It remains to be seen whether the most popular professional sport in other countries catches on here.

Here comes the "ZooChoo"! The steam locomotive, which hauls three fringe-topped cars, is a scaled down model of an 1863 vintage. The train runs on an 1800-foot right of way through the Children's Zoo.

Betsy, the chimpanzee, absorbed in her art. During her career (1954-1957) her canvases sold for a total of $4,500, and found buyers as far away as Australia.

Two other popular features of the Children's Zoo are the Noah's Ark (above) and the Rabbit House (below) with its carrot and lettuce motif.

All Aboard for the "ZooChoo"!

A FAVORITE RESORT for young and old is the Baltimore Zoo, in Druid Hill Park. Here one finds a collection of over 1000 specimens of animals, birds and reptiles. A welcome addition is the Children's Zoo, opened in the spring of 1963. Among other things it houses kittens, puppies, donkeys, ponies, calves and kids, and a barnyard where city children can get acquainted with such rarities as live cows, chickens and ducks. Then there is the "ZooChoo", a miniature train with steam engine and cars. The Zoo has had some notable inmates. Remember Betsy, the artist, whose paintings were famous in this country and abroad?

The Johns Hopkins University campus at Homewood, on North Charles Street, as seen from the air. Here is the Faculty of Arts and Sciences, with its graduate and undergraduate bodies; and also the Evening College.

At the Johns Hopkins
Quality, Not Size, is the Goal

"OUR STRENGTH cannot be in numbers. It must be in excellence." Thus spoke Dr. Milton Eisenhower at his inauguration as President of the Johns Hopkins University, on February 22, 1957. The problem of the next ten years was that of meeting overwhelming demands by sustained quality rather than size.

In many parts of this country and in distant lands, Baltimore is best known as the home of the Hopkins Medical School and Hospital; for the training of graduate and undergraduate students on the Homewood campus; for its School of Advanced International Studies in Washington, with the overseas division in Bologna, Italy; and for the space research and development at its Applied Physics Laboratory in Howard County.

While the faculty and student body have remained small in comparison to other American universities, new departments have been added, accompanied by an ambitious building program. The goal of sustained excellence, announced by Dr. Eisenhower, is being pursued by his successor, Dr. Lincoln Gordon.

Above, Dr. Eisenhower (left) retiring President, congratulates his successor, Dr. Gordon (right) as Harvard's President Nathan M. Pusey looks on. Below, the catamaran *Ridgely Warfield* engages in the university's oceanographic research.

162

Above, the old hospital flanked on the left by the new John F. Kennedy Institute for the rehabilitation of handicapped children. Rising in the rear is the new Children's Medical and Surgical Center. At right, the Eisenhower Library at Homewood.

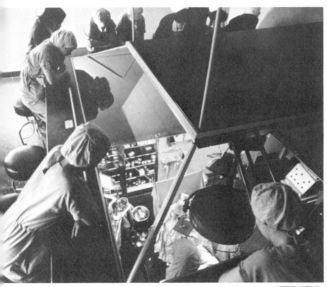

Students of the School of Nursing look through glass panels at an operation being performed on the floor below. These future "R.N's" are trained to assume large responsibilities.

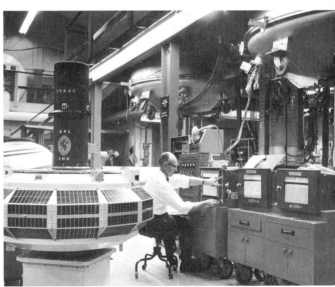

A scientist at work in the Applied Physics Laboratory. Here in 1958 was begun space research and development leading to the launching of navigational satellites that have revolutionized the art of navigation.

Education Meets the Population Explosion Head-On

BRICKS AND MORTAR may not make a university; but they, or their equivalent in stone and mortar, help. The bumper crop of boys and girls, born in the past two decades and clamoring for education, has called for a massive program of construction from elementary schools to colleges. Old institutions in the Baltimore area have been expanded and new ones have been founded. An innovation has been the rise of junior colleges, both public and private, offering two year courses, such as the Community College of Baltimore, Essex Community College and Catonsville Community College. While movement has been toward the suburbs there now are plans for campuses in the inner city. Conspicuous among them is that of the graduate schools of the University of Maryland. Award for ingenuity should go to the Maryland Institute for turning a railroad station into an art studio.

164

Above, College Center Courtyard on Goucher's 425-acre campus at Towson. Below, the B. & O.'s Mount Royal Station converted into an annex of the Maryland Institute.

At left, the new home of Baltimore Polytechnic Institute and Western High School, at Falls Road and Cold Spring Lane. Below, the Community College of Baltimore, on Liberty Heights Avenue.

Center, the University of Maryland's downtown campus project. The new Law School building (not shown) is complete. Planned are buildings for the Dental School and School of Nursing.

Above left, grounds of Morgan State College, with the auditorium in the background. Right, not a school for golfers, but students at Towson State College relaxing between classes.

165

Above, the new Protestant Episcopal Church of the Redeemer, on North Charles Street, completed in 1958, serves a growing parish founded in 1855.

At right, First Christian Church, on Roland Avenue. This hexagonal structure has its altar in the center.

Religious Growth Keeps Pace with the Secular

IN THIS MATERIALISTIC AGE some cynics have said that God is dead. If so, it is passing strange that in the Baltimore community so many new houses of worship are being raised in His honor. These churches and temples have, for the most part, followed their congregations to the suburbs. On the whole, the boldness and originality of the designs are representative of our contemporary architecture, rather than a repetition of conventional patterns, as the examples selected for these pages illustrate.

Of all the religious edifices erected during the past decade, by far the most ambitious is the new Roman Catholic cathedral. It is unique among cathedrals in that it was completed within a few years and that it was the gift of a single individual.

Grace Lutheran Church, in Lutherville. The architect has skillfully combined nave and steeple.

Roman Catholic Cathedral of Mary Our Queen, on North Charles Street. It was dedicated November 5, 1959.

Temple Oheb Shalom, on Park Heights Avenue. The four arches suggest the Tablets of the Laws, or Ten Commandments.

Above, The Dundalk Marine Terminal, covering 365 acres, is one of the most modern on the East Coast. Here the foreign cars are landed, and here are facilities for handling containers, while marginal piers provide berths for seven or eight ships at a time.

At left, a map showing the Patapsco River and the inner harbor. The black areas mark the locations of most of the piers and main marine complexes.

Baltimore's Link with the Ports of the World

THE MARYLAND PORT AUTHORITY was established in 1957 to increase waterborne commerce by developing existing facilities and by advertising those facilities at home and abroad. It can point to an outstanding record of achievement. Facilities have been expanded and methods of servicing vessels and handling cargoes made to conform with the latest and most economic practices.

Baltimore receives more than 5200 ships a year. It is connected with more than 291 ports of the world by 90 berthline steamship services flying the flags of 47 nations, not counting 13 steamship lines servicing specialized bulk cargoes. Over a 20-year period the cargoes handled—foreign, coastal and intercoastal—have averaged 48 million tons a year. The port's pier and cargo facilities include 94 piers, open and covered, which can handle 171 vessels at once.

The importation of automobiles from abroad has been one of its leading operations. In 1966 a total of 146,000 foreign cars passed through the port, giving Baltimore the undisputed title of No. 1 U.S. port of entry that year.

But Baltimore's port is not all general and bulk cargoes. More colorful are the popular Caribbean cruises which set sail from here, not to speak of the good ship *Port Welcome* whose course is confined to home waters.

Above, an ore boat ties up at the Bethlehem Steel Company. The 4000-acre Sparrows Point plant operates the largest tidewater ore dock in the world. It is 2200 feet long, is equipped with ten cranes, and has berthing space for three carriers up to 50,000 tons. Bethlehem is the largest employer in Baltimore.

Above, a giant gantry crane picks up containers from 20 to 40 feet long, and loads or unloads them. This "roll on-roll off" system has gained wide popularity. It saves labor and reduces pilferage.

At left, above. The *Port Welcome* with a local party aboard pleasure-bound down the Bay. It also is handy in entertaining the Authority's visitors.

At left, below. The cruise ship *Argentina*, about to set sail for the Caribbean, under the auspices of Maryland Cruises Inc., set up in 1962. Since then over 13,000 passengers have embarked.

The $30,000,000 plant of the Kennecott Refining Corporation at Hawkins Point, where copper from Chile is refined. At far right is the Glidden Company, paint manufacturers.

Another large industrial park. This one, the Meadows, lies off the Beltway and adjoins the Social Security complex.

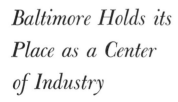

A view of Camden Industrial Park, significant in that it lies in the downtown area, convenient to railroads, highways and the homes of workers.

At Towson, Parke Davis & Company, drug manufacturers, is typical of the attractively housed light industry plants appearing along the Beltway.

Baltimore Holds its Place as a Center of Industry

IN THE PRESENT PERIOD of population growth and economic expansion Baltimore maintains its traditional position as one of the leading industrial centers of the nation. Located here are such giants as Bethlehem Steel, whose normal pay-roll is 30,000; Western Electric, second largest employer, with 16,000 workers in its 21 separate plants and offices, and Kennecott Refining Corporation, whose plant at Hawkins Point refines copper both for domestic and foreign manufacture.

170

The Greater Baltimore Industrial Park, largest of this type of production unit, lies in Baltimore County, just off the Baltimore-Harrisburg Expressway. It covers 450 acres and is composed of 22 firms employing 7000 people. The structure in the foreground is a high-rise office building, the first of four that will range in height from 10 to 15 stories. A motel and restaurant are added features.

One of Westinghouse's many local plants. The company, having made radar for Project Gemini, is to supply instruments for the moon astronauts.

A new and important development is the industrial park where a number of industries are grouped together in a center convenient to electric power, transportation and the various other facilities essential to production. During the last decade as many as sixty, both large and small, have been established in the metropolitan district. Added to all these are the many attractively designed light industry plants which are springing up along the Beltway.

A close-up of the high-rise office building in the Greater Baltimore Industrial Park. The park is one of three local projects of Maryland Properties, Inc., which is its own builder and the largest developer of industrial parks in the east.

171

MAPS, INCORPORATED

MARION E. WARREN

Above, a view of Mount Royal Plaza showing the State Office, State Roads, and State Employment Security Buildings.

At left, the Social Security complex, spread over 140 acres, where some 12,000 employees process the nation's more than 200 million listings.

Below, in this 17-story structure in Charles Center, are housed 15 Federal agencies employing 2,250 persons.

Handsome Homes of State and Federal Agencies

BECAUSE IT IS the metropolis of Maryland, and because of its proximity to the national capital, Baltimore is ideally located as a home for government agencies, both State and Federal. For the sake of convenience, it has been the rule to concentrate operations in a single area or building. Thus Mount Royal Plaza has been developed as a center of Maryland government agencies. Similarly agencies of the national government have been assembled in the spacious Federal Building in Charles Center. That Baltimore is well suited to serve as a national headquarters is exemplified by the great Social Security complex, in Woodlawn, west Baltimore.

A. AUBREY BODINE

The "Trafficopter". It also covers Stadium game traffic and other special events.

An architect's rendering of ETV's Baltimore station soon to rise at Owings Mills.

"For Your Information"

TYPICAL OF THE AGE are the strides made in communication through radio and television illustrated on this page. Tallest object in Maryland, rising 1000 feet above ground on a hill at Woodberry, is the lithe "candelabra" television tower. Completed in September, 1964, and owned by three local stations, it sends signals to six states.

The "Trafficopter", sponsored by Radio Station WFBR and manned by the city Department of Transit and Traffic, soars above the highways morning and evening warning motorists of tie-ups.

Due to begin in 1969 is Maryland's Educational Television which will broadcast educational programs on a special ETV network.

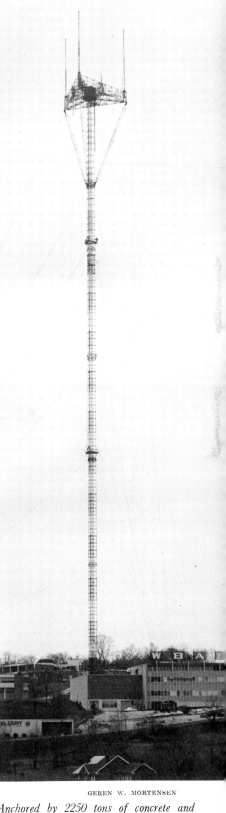

Anchored by 2250 tons of concrete and 5½ miles of steel guy wire, the "candelabra" tower is designed to withstand winds of 165 miles an hour.

Better Housing is a Vital Factor in Urban Renewal

LESS SPECTACULAR than Charles Center, but equally important in reviving the inner city, is the program for providing decent housing and living conditions for people of all income levels. This is being carried out under the direction of the Baltimore Urban Renewal and Housing Agency. Typical is Harlem Park. Here some old houses were razed and replaced by apartments; others were restored, while unsightly alleys were transformed into inviting parks. Essential to the program has been the cooperation of the residents, represented by the Harlem Park Neighborhood Council. At the other end of the scale are dwellings, designed for the higher income group, for which BURHA supplied the sites.

SUNPAPERS

These houses, too far gone to be restored, are being torn down to make way for apartments equipped with all modern improvements.

MARION E. WARREN

Bolton Place. These charming town houses for persons in the higher income brackets replaced a fast deteriorating neighborhood.

BALTIMORE URBAN RENEWAL AND HOUSING AGENCY

The George B. Murphy Homes, a part of the Harlem Park Area project, contains 750 low rent dwelling units, including a number for senior citizens.

Before renewal. This dreary waste of bare ground and trash is what Harlem Park alleys looked like.

PLAY AREA
FOR
CHILDREN
Under 14 Years Old

And here is one of the inviting parks that replaced the alleys. Plenty of room for play free of traffic hazards.

Laying bricks. These youngsters set an example in community cooperation.

175

Six Monuments Undergo a Face Lifting

PROGRESS is not always good. Sometimes in its haste to advance it tramples things in its path that are worth preserving. Fortunately for Baltimore there have always been many among its citizens who, while looking to the future, venerate old landmarks and work hard to save them from destruction.

Here are presented six striking examples of restoration, or tidying up, that have been carried out simultaneously with the rebuilding of the inner city. They include a wide variety of structures—an ancient warship, a synagogue, a Quaker meeting house, the former home of a nun

of the Roman Catholic Church whose life of sacrifice and good deeds has marked her out for sainthood, and the city residence of a Maryland signer of the Declaration of Independence.

While the work on Monument Square is not strictly a restoration the addition of the garden plot of shrubs and trees approaches one. The embellishment may serve to discourage the periodic threat to move the monument in order to speed the flow of traffic. Scene of many mass meetings in early days, and of the annual observances of the Battle of North Point, the square is one of the most historic spots in the city.

The U.S. *Frigate Constellation*, at her pier in the inner harbor. The oldest American warship afloat, she was in active service during World War II, during which she was flagship of the Atlantic Fleet. Restoration was largely financed by the sale of 350,000 coins containing copper from original spikes, at a dollar each.

This handsome house was the city residence of Charles Carroll of Carrollton, Maryland signer. He died here in 1832, at the age of 95 years.

Monument Square today. The monument commemorates Baltimore's heroic part in the War of 1812.

Friends' Old Town Meeting House, at Aisquith and Fayette Streets, was built in 1781. Abandoned in the 1920's, it was restored in 1967.

Above, Lloyd Street Synagogue, the first synagogue to be built in Maryland. Below, 600 North Paca Street, occupied in 1808-9 by Blessed Elizabeth Ann Seton, foundress of the Daughters of Charity in the United States.

The Oyster Roast. It begins at the raw bar, then progresses to oysters roasted, fried or frittered; along with "all the fixin's."

A. AUBREY BODINE

The Crab Feast. Eating hard-shell crabs calls for manual dexterity, good eyesight and deep concentration. No time to "look pleasant!"

SUNPAPERS

Below, a frying pan loaded with crab cakes. After a few minutes over the fire they will be ready to titillate the palate of a gourmet.

SUNPAPERS

"Moco" Yardley's Crab Cakes

(The genial Sunpapers' cartoonist is also a recognized gourmet.)

1 lb. crab meat	½ tsp. pepper
1 slice of bread	1 tbsp. mayonnaise
1 beaten egg	1 tbsp. dry mustard
1 tsp. salt	1 tbsp. parsley

Break bread into small pieces. Mix well into ingredients. Put in crab meat last so as to break it up as little as possible. Make into about six cakes and fry in bacon fat—or, for calorie counters, place on cookie tin and bake in oven. Worcestershire sauce may be added to mixture, if you wish.

GEREN W. MORTENSEN

At left, a Marine guard mount according to 1812 regulations. A weekly event in summer at Fort McHenry.

Below, at left, the first Greater Baltimore Arts Festival in Charles Center, which may become an annual affair.

Below, an open air art exhibit, where local artists show their works to potential buyers.

MARION E. WARREN

SUNPAPERS

Food, Fads and Fancies

ALMOST A CENTURY AGO Dr. Oliver Wendell Holmes dubbed Baltimore "the gastronomical center of the universe." Times have changed, and such local delicacies as canvas-back ducks and diamond-back terrapin are harder to come by. Nevertheless there remains a substantial basis for the claim, especially during the seasons for oyster roasts and crab feasts. They are as popular as ever,

whether for sociability, to foster the interests of a political party, or to help a charitable cause. But it would be a mistake to assume that the local public is completely absorbed with food. There are other diversions appealing to a variety of tastes— from watching a guard mount at Fort McHenry, to patronizing open air art shows—at festivals by lakes, fountains or railroad tracks.

179

At right, the "Golden Triangle." New high-rise apartments spring up beside old apartments on West University Parkway. Below, 222 St. Paul Street, combined office and apartment building in the heart of downtown.

Garden apartments, limited to two or three floors in height, are a compromise for those who would preserve some of the quality of a house.

"More Stately Mansions" Rising Toward the Skies

On the left. The complex of high-rise apartments in a sylvan setting in the suburbs, with ample space for swimming pools and parking, contains all the ingredients for luxurious living. On the right, Roland View Towers East, is church sponsored. Apartments are available only to elderly persons of moderate means.

IT IS FINE to have a house of one's own. But there are irksome responsibilities, such as upkeep, insurance and protection during the owner's absence. Why not escape them by turning them over to somebody else? For many people the answer is an apartment; especially for those who suddenly realize they are not as young as they were. Now that, thanks to advances in preventive medicine, more senior citizens are around, the demand for apartments has burgeoned.

Apartments are nothing new; but characteristic of the present era are "high-rise" apartments, some of which soar upwards twenty floors and more. They are to be found both in the suburbs and in the center of the city. A number, sponsored by religious groups, are designed primarily for the elderly. But the "high-rise" does not have the field to itself. Popular also are apartments built in groups, limited in height to two or three floors, and retaining the flavor of private houses.

These gracious houses are on John Street, in the heart of Bolton Hill. Three quarters of a century or more old, they are designed to give abundant room and light. Garden space was obtained by blocking off the street.

Some Bold Spirits Refuse to Desert the City

NOT EVERYONE who could afford the move has fled the city. Many have remained in old residential neighborhoods in order to enjoy the advantages the inner city offers. To provide themselves with comfortable living quarters they have undertaken what has been called "Do-it-yourself renewal." That is, without public help, they have remodeled old houses with charming results. Nowhere has this been better done than in Tyson Street and the Bolton Hill area.

Above, one of the refurbished row houses characteristic of the city at the turn of the century. At right, most colorful of all— Tyson Street.

Twenty Million Passengers at Friendship by 1985

FRIENDSHIP AIRPORT, preparing to take care of the growth in air travel forecast for the years immediately ahead, is planning a massive program of expansion. It proposes to serve 20,000,000 passengers a year by 1985. Total cost of new construction and other improvements is estimated at $400,000,000. Supersonic and "Jumbo" planes designed to carry 600 passengers each, too large to be serviced in the present restricted area, will be provided with individual satellite stations. Passengers will use moving walks to reach them from the main terminal. Other proposed facilities include parking space for 18,000 cars.

At top, a view of Friendship Airport as it is today, looking toward the main terminal with the entrance road and parking lot in the foreground. Below, a model of the airport of the future. Note the satellite stations for supersonic planes at far right. They will require twice as much space as the largest planes of today.

183

A model of the Inner Harbor Project I, showing the motel and marinas on the water on the west, the Maryland Port Authority Building on the north and the Christ Lutheran Church center and playing fields on the south. A bridge carries the East-West Expressway to Federal Hill.

Inner Harbor Project I and other Future Plans

THE URBAN RENEWAL program moves on. Scheduled to begin in 1968 is Inner Harbor Project I. Covering 85 acres around three sides of the harbor basin, it will provide for office buildings, apartments, a motel, marinas, restaurant, theaters, parks and public institutions. The Maryland Port Authority will erect an international trade center; the Maryland Academy of Sciences plans a building,

and Christ Lutheran Church a complex including a house of worship, apartments for the elderly, a nursing home and recreation space.

Among other major improvements, the city will see new piers at Locust Point and a $16,000,000 main Post Office. Most ambitious of all is the proposed rapid transit system to bring people from the suburbs to the city at high speed.

MARYLAND PORT AUTHORITY

SUNPAPERS

WESTINGHOUSE ELECTRIC CORP.

At left, an architect's drawing of the new piers at Locust Point, to cost over $2,000,000 and provide four deep water berths, a storage shed and container facilities. Below, the 35-story Maryland Port Authority building which will house the international trade center.

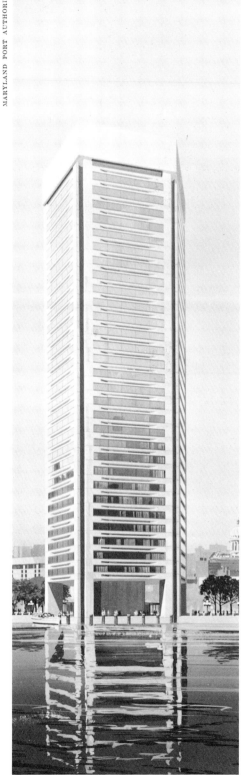

In the middle, above, a drawing of the new main Post Office which will occupy a 12-acre site bounded by Fayette, Front, Low and Colvin Streets. Directly above, cars and tracks like these might be used on the proposed rapid transit system, radiating from Charles Center. Trains would run every two minutes around the clock, and the 12.8 miles from Randallstown to the Center would be covered in 21 minutes.

ACKNOWLEDGMENTS

WE ARE MOST GRATEFUL to the following organizations and individuals for their kind cooperation in lending valued pictures and supplying helpful information for this book:

Bachrach
Balmoral Towers
Baltimore and Ohio Railroad (affiliated
    with the Chesapeake and Ohio Railway)
Baltimore Ballet Company
Baltimore Chapter, American Red Cross
Baltimore Civic Opera Company
Baltimore Clippers
Baltimore Gas and Electric Company
Baltimore Magazine
Baltimore Museum of Art
Baltimore News American
Baltimore Orioles Baseball Club, Inc.
Baltimore Urban Renewal and Housing
    Agency
Baltimore Zoo
Blakeslee-Lane
Chamber of Commerce of Metropolitan
    Baltimore
Chesapeake and Potomac Telephone Co.
Community College of Baltimore
Department of Traffic and Transit
Emerson Drug Company
Enoch Pratt Free Library
Equitable Trust Company
Mr. H. Findlay French
The Flag House
Goucher College
Greater Baltimore Committee
Greater Baltimore Medical Center
Mr. Alexander Brown Griswold
Hamlet West Apartments

Hughes Company
Hutzler Archives
Johns Hopkins Hospital
Johns Hopkins University
Mrs. C. C. Knobeloch
Mr. Harry B. Leopold
Library of Congress
Loyola College
Maps, Incorporated
Maryland Educational Television
    Commission
Maryland Jockey Club
Maryland Port Authority
Maryland Properties, Inc.
Morris A. Mechanic Theatre
Mergenthaler Vocational High School
Mr. Robert G. Merrick
Peabody Institute
Peale Museum
Mr. G. H. Pouder
Roland View Towers
J. H. Schaefer & Son
Dr. Harry R. Slack
Smithsonian Institution
Sunpapers
Two Twenty Two St. Paul
University of Maryland
U.S. Air Force
U.S. Coast Guard
Walters Art Gallery
Westinghouse Electric Corporation
WFBR

A special word of appreciation should be extended to the following individuals: Mr. G. H. Pouder, Executive Vice-President (retired), the Chamber of Commerce of Metropolitan Baltimore; Mr. Earl Pruce, Librarian, *Baltimore News-American*; Miss Elizabeth Litsinger, Head of the Maryland Department (retired), Enoch Pratt Free Library; Mr. Wilbur H. Hunter, Jr., Director, Peale Museum and Mr. Charles H. Elam, Archivist; and Mr. Clement Vitek, Chief Librarian, *Sunpapers*.

HAROLD R. MANAKEE, *Director, the Maryland Historical Society*

FRANCIS F. BEIRNE, *Author*

The front end paper, Baltimore in the 1850's, is from an engraving at the Maryland Historical Society. The back end paper, Baltimore in the 1960's, reproduces a photograph of a similar view a century and a decade later, courtesy of Maps, Incorporated.

The frontispiece is a view of Baltimore in the 1940's, from the files of Blakeslee-Lane.